CHRONOLOGICAL ORDER

CHRONOLOGICAL ORDER

THE FINE PRINT FOR A LARGE LIFE

JILL B. YESKO & LAUREAN KILE

DISCOVER ORGANIZING PRESS

Copyright © 2021 by Jill B. Yesko & Laurean Kile

No part of this publication shall be reproduced, transmitted, or sold in whole or in part in any form without prior written consent of both authors, except as provided by the United States of America copyright law. Any unauthorized usage of the text without express written permission of the publisher is a violation of the authors' copyright and is illegal and punishable by law. All trademarks and registered trademarks appearing in this text are the property of their respective owners.

For permission requests, write to the below address:

Jill B. Yesko
Discover Organizing Inc.
98 Vanadium Road, Building D
Bridgeville, PA 15017

Ordering Information: Quantity sales and special discounts are available on quantity purchases by corporations, associations, and others. For details, contact the author at jill@discoverorganizing.com.

Edited by: Andrea Glass
Cover design by: Nathan C. Yesko
Illustrations by: Nathan C. Yesko
Typeset by: Medlar Publishing Solutions Pvt. Ltd., India and Ethan Earlewine
Photo credit: Anita Buzzy Prentiss

Printed in the United States of America

ISBN: 978-0-578883-73-1 (print)
ISBN: 978-0-578883-74-8 (ebook)

Library of Congress Control Number: 2021916825

First Edition: December, 2021

The information contained within this book is strictly for informational purposes. The material may include information, products, or services by third parties. As such, the Authors and Publisher do not assume responsibility or liability for any third-party material or opinions. The publisher is not responsible for websites (or their content) that are not owned by the publisher.

All rights reserved. The illustrations within this book may not be reproduced or used in any manner whatsoever without the express written permission of the Illustrator.

To my family and friends, and in memory of my father, William J. Banmiller - Jill B. Yesko

This book is dedicated to the memory of William W. Kile. Thanks William for inspiring me to pursue living each day on earth as it is in heaven and to my children, Kailyn, Evign and Eyan who motivate me to never stop living this way! - Laurean Kile

Contents

Introduction 1

Your Twenties 7

Your Thirties 39

Your Forties 67

Your Fifties 87

Your Sixties 113

Your Seventies 133

Your Eighties. 165

Your Nineties 181

The Life Essentials 193

Resources 225

Sources. 227

Afterword 231

CHRONOLOGICAL ORDER

ABOUT THE AUTHORS: JILL B. YESKO 233

ABOUT THE AUTHORS: LAUREAN KILE 234

ACKNOWLEDGEMENTS 236

INDEX 240

Introduction

Chronological Order

When Heidi Murkoff wrote *What to Expect When You're Expecting* in 1984, it quickly became a national bestseller. In 2012 the book was made into a movie starring Cameron Diaz and Jennifer Lopez (Lionsgate). The bookstore shelves were rapidly emptied of this pre-Google pregnancy bible by expecting parents, grandparents, and friends of the parents-to-be. Everyone wanted to follow along with a pregnancy week by week, and month by month, anticipating with first-hand knowledge what each phase of those nine months would feel like (and look like). There's even a section to address the often-overlooked part of pregnancy, the postpartum phase. I had a copy during my first pregnancy and read it often, and sometimes even read ahead. I couldn't wait to see what would happen. Reading that book was like binge-watching back-to-back episodes of myself in The Nature Channel with a VR headset in today's standards. I mean, this was really happening to me, and it was so...accurate!

When Laurean Kile and I decided to write *this* book, we discovered that we were writing something similar, but about what actually happens after turning 20. We were imagining it being a valuable and practical tool for people who are aging—which is basically everyone on the planet. We considered putting pictures of people aging in the book, decade by decade, but honestly, it's not necessarily a comforting set of images. I mean, it might have stopped people from reading the next chapter, and that's somewhat antithetical. Chapter inserts titled, "Your 60s: More Wrinkles Appear" (see inset photo of a woman in 60s frowning in a mirror) wouldn't encourage our readers or help us sell more books. We were also considering starting with your 90s and working your way backward, like a wayward tribute to Benjamin Button. Still, we ultimately decided to start this book when we hoped people would pick it up for the first time: *in their 20s*.

I mostly called my parents for advice during that decade, but something tells me that if they had this book back then, they would have just sent it to me, along with a highlighter, and told me to stop calling them (especially my mother; I think I taxed her the most). I still argue that advice was cheaper than sending me money, but writing a check might have been easier for them than to listen to me agonize about yet another fork in my winding, uphill, and rocky road of adulting.

If you're picking up this book at 67, 34, 82, or 56, or **any age**, we promise it's a good time to do it. We tucked tips and helpful advice into each chapter that are relevant for every phase of living, like

INTRODUCTION

how to organize paper piles, manage daily clutter, and financial and legal tips. Laurean and I spent separate careers in our more recent decades helping older adults. She was a Senior Advisor and advocate, and I'm a Senior Move Manager and Professional Organizer. As the content developed, we soon realized that this book was for people who were never given a manual on how to not only manage being *alive* but to possibly get the most out of the time they're given. (So it's actually written for everyone—unless you got a manual somehow. We didn't!)

Oh, how I wish I'd been given this manual years ago! It would have better prepared me for life's curveballs and saved me hours of research in my work as a Senior Advisor. Working with tens of thousands of aging adults and their families, many of whom needed or were receiving end-of-life care, I had to learn a lot, and now we get to impart it all to you!

My work as a Senior Advisor, surrounded by people who were nearing the end of their journey on this planet, was a gift. I was given the looking glass into the future, and what came into focus was that at the end of our lives there are those who leave this earth filled with regret and those who leave feeling very satisfied with a life well-lived. I want the latter for you!

Just like Jill says, you can open this book and find the essential information you'll need to be prepared and plan for the years ahead, no matter your age. If you picked up this book and you're still in your 20s, WOW, you're amazing! I wish I were as bright as you when I was at your age. It honestly took me coming up on my 50s before I became more determined to plan for myself to age successfully.

That's what this book is all about. It will cause you to think, plan, dream, and prepare, and my prayer is that it will prompt you to take action to thrive through each decade of your life! Jill and I share our own experiences and the wisdom and struggles of the countless families we've helped along the way. The pages of this book have truly evolved into a Life Manual. Tucked inside, you'll find everything we wished we'd known or what our clients needed to take care of while we helped them. We're thrilled you've decided to pick up a copy, and we know you'll be so much more prepared to create one fantastic life for yourself.

Chronological Order

There are elements of this book that will be consistently included. In every chapter, we'll cover:

- **Your Identity and Well-being**
- **Your Home and Your Space**
- **Your Financial and Professional Goals**
- **Your Relationships and Social Life**

At the end of every chapter is a checklist of all you MUST have in place at any age. We call these your Life Essentials. We will be placing the **Life Essentials** list at the end of each chapter to make sure that we are reminding the reader about the importance of We will also go into more detail about each Life Essential in the last chapter! The Life Essentials are:

- **Life Insurance**
- **Will**
- **Living Will**
- **Vital Records Organization**
- **Power of Attorney**
- **Home Inventory**
- **Health Benefits**
- **Care and Living Plan**

At various points throughout the book, you'll find:

Reality Checks
These are poignant revelations and reminders that we think are the most essential "truths" to be told by us (because we know best and are basically geniuses).

Storytime
This icon, when seen throughout the book, indicates an anecdotal departure or two. If you don't like amazingly relevant human-interest stories, breeze past these.

INTRODUCTION

Yield to You
These little signs are messages that you need to respect about yourself. They're moments for those who feel like they might not precisely fit the archetype or typical patterns of their generation or normal phases depicted by the decade they're currently living.

And some additional themes are woven into various decades to make this book more appealing. They are:

Photographic Memories
Everyone takes pictures. These tips are brought to you to help get photos and memorabilia under control and for them to become more meaningful.

About Your Parents
These sections address what happens when our own parents age and the concerns and challenges this might bring to you and your family.

Finally, since there are two authors with very different styles and personalities, we'll tell you who's talking with these icons:

YOUR TWENTIES

CHRONOLOGICAL ORDER

Your Identity and Well-being

To those in their 20s: "Adulting" has begun!

Welcome! You made it through your teens and are now just embarking on living your own life. How exciting is this time in your life?! I know it's hard to think of yourself as being old one day, especially since you're probably just finishing up college, starting your first job, or perhaps have fallen deeply in love for the first time. Humor me a moment and imagine yourself at the end of your life. How does that look? Take some time to imagine your life 50, 60, 70+ years from now. Get a good mental picture. Do you like what you see?

We're all aging, and you're no longer a kid!

The choices you make in your 20s can form a firm foundation for you to have one wonderful, complete, and satisfying life! What kind of life do you want to live? What future do you dream of? What will your story be? I was once in a business networking meeting, and a sage woman said these words that had a profound effect on me. She said, "If you're going to set any goals, you might as well DREAM IT UP BIG."

So, take the time now to write down those big dreams and goals. Step back and think about how much it's going to cost to create this life. What skills do you need to learn, and what actions can you take today to reach them? Now is the time to be a bit selfish, to believe in yourself, and to create the life you desire! A healthy mindset and focus are vital to living your life to the fullest. There's nothing you can't do if you believe in yourself and take intentional action toward your dreams each day.

It's not difficult to have one wonderful life as you age if you're intentional about it. One of my abilities I'm most passionate about now is helping others uncover their gifts, talents, and ideas they have inside of them. I've embraced my own gift to help others live to their full potential. A few years ago, I created the Launch Collective Mastermind, where a group of entrepreneurs gathers to help accelerate each other's business growth. I now host the Launch Collective EXPO, online workshops, and work one-on-one consulting as a Professional Encourager.

One of the first exercises I work on with my clients is for them to create an Intentional Life Map. Typically, a life map is a visual timeline from the day you were born until the present day. It's a tool to document where you've come from up until the present. What I have my clients do is create an Intentional Life Map that has them put on paper all the steps it will take to live the life they imagine in the future. It's an effective exercise and brings out deep desires and the limiting beliefs and fears that may be holding them back from taking action. I highly encourage you to do this!

Here are five simple steps to create your Intentional Life Map, get yourself a nice journal and get started:

Step 1: Dream it Up Big! What are your heart's desires? You have to have a vision for your life. **START DREAMING!** *What do you desire to have? What do you desire to do? Where do you desire to go, see, live, experience? If money were no object, you would... Write everything down here!*

Step 2: Assessment. *How are you doing today in these critical areas of your life? Are you lacking in any?*
- Family & Relationships
- Health & Wellness
- Finances
- Career & Business
- Social Life & Hobbies
- Spiritual Life
- Education & Mentors

Step 3: Finish this sentence: I will and must achieve my goals because... *(what is your why???)*

Step 4: Write down your goals and plot your future timeline. (i.e., one year from now I will..., five years from now I will..., ten years from now I will...). Writing out your goals is powerful! Most of the highly successful people in the world write down their most important goals on paper each day!

Step 5: Take ACTION! What's one step you can take today to bring you closer to what you just wrote down? Without action, your DREAM will remain just that, a dream. Take ACTION and believe in your ability. If you can THINK it, you can DO IT!

This exercise also helps you discover more about yourself through your twenties. It helps you to see more clearly your own identity, the amazing person you are. No matter how old you are or where you are today, you have the ability to create a better future for yourself. It all starts with an idea and a written plan. You see this concept called time—it passes by us very quickly the older we get. Don't wait for a better time, or tell yourself, "one day when I'm older... or when I have X, Y & Z, then I'll do it." Do NOT listen to that voice.... GO for it; there's no better time than now!

With greater independence comes greater responsibility.

This sounds pretty compelling, but that's because it is. The more you break free from your parents, the more decisions you'll have to make on your own. Breaking free from the bonds of your parents sounded all fine and good when you were 15 and still weren't allowed to go on dates or didn't get a cell phone or weren't permitted to stay out past 11 P.M. "When I get my own place, I'm going to do whatever I want, whenever I want!" Maybe you had to do chores, like mop the kitchen floor and clean the bathrooms once a week. If you had siblings, perhaps you divided your chores on some type of chart that hung in the kitchen (my mom laminated ours and rotated the lists to keep it interesting from week to week). Being on your own sounded pretty darn good! Freedom!

You can watch TV whenever you want, with the volume as loud as you please, and if you're going to eat Doritos after 10 P.M. and not brush your teeth, so what? How about staying at the popular kids' parties until 2:00 A.M., huh? Yep, that would be awesome!

Well, if you're in your 20s and on your own, in that apartment—roommate or no—you're discovering how great that freedom is! If you work or go to school (and work), you probably think that sleep is incredible if you can get it, and the bathroom floors need to be done, but so does the grocery shopping. Let's not forget the dog that doesn't walk itself, and the Netflix shows that everyone else is binge-watching on weekends are far out of reach with your schedule. Besides, Netflix might sound expensive to you if money is tight, and Doritos are a brand-name chip you can enjoy the generic counterpart of "just fine." Here's a list of facts I discovered in my first new place, on my very own:

Toilet Paper Truth: When it's gone, it's gone. No one magically replaces the rolls under the bathroom sink. Huh?
The Stuff on the Floor: If it sticks to your bare feet, it's dirt, and NO ONE will sweep it up or mop it up but you.
The dog: Food, walks, let-outs, clean-ups, playing, vet visits—it's all you, man, all you.
Food: The cabinets, fridge, and pantry will not automatically refill when you consume food or dirty your dishes. I'm sorry.
Laundry: You might guess this one—when the clothes are dirty, they just pile up. It's weird!

In *my* 20s, I wore more hats in one decade than any other in my life. I was a college grad, a new mother, then a new Army wife (yes, in that order), and working as a Case Manager for a mental health center. I was also taking care of my wonderful and sweet grandmother when I was 17 until I was 24. I moved to Panama (yes, the country) then Pittsburgh, PA, with my new little family when I was 25 and had my second child at 26. We went from my mother-in-law's home to a condo, then onto a rented larger house, all within two years. At 28, I filed for a divorce and went back to work as a Case Manager in my new, unfamiliar town, sticking my little ones in daycare, and quickly fell into a new career in human resources. At 30, I had taken a new job as an HR Director, and my kids (now five and seven) and I moved into my own home that I bought with my own money.

One of the signs that you're maturing is when you're job hunting, you may be more interested in the group health plan than their vacation benefits. The hours you work are most likely long, as you're trying to prove yourself in your new career and making sure you don't fail. You're juggling a busy schedule, and you might feel like you'll "never catch up."

This is the time to build the foundation for lifelong habits! This is the time!!!

Okay, I'm being dramatic because the "I wish I would have" people I meet and work with tell me, in their regretful, somewhat angry way, "If only I had learned this early on! I wish someone would have taught me this in my youth! Why didn't I listen to my parents?? I feel like I never really knew what I was doing back then (in my 20s)!" Sigh. This is the rub. Hindsight is 20/20. I know, I know. But if you're in your 20s, I really want you to pay attention. Like right now.

Create the routines that will give you structure with your time and your environment and allow you enough freedom to enjoy your personal time. I'm not saying you have to do laundry every Saturday and meal planning every Sunday, like most of the working world. What's important is establishing a routine that keeps you organized and feeling like you're simplifying your life for YOU and anyone else who lives with you. Here are some examples of a daily routine that might work for you:

It's Monday, so...
6:00 A.M. - *Wake, work out, eat*
7:00 A.M. - *Shower, dress, prepare for the workday (check emails for any changes to your schedule)*
8:00 A.M. - *Leave for work, or school, or whatever it is that you do*
9:00 A.M. - *Do what you do for money, education, fitness, socialization, family, etc., la, la, la, la, la, la (you're doing it)*
5:00 P.M. - *Come home, cook, eat (work out or exercise if you didn't this morning)*
6:00 P.M. - *Do one load of laundry* and while you're waiting for the machines to do their thing...*

7:00 P.M. - *Do one of the chores needed around the house (vacuuming, sorting mail, etc.)*
7:30 P.M. - *Finish laundry*
8:00 P.M. - *Prepare for the next day (get clothes and lunch ready; lay out everything you need to take with you; pack your work bag, and put by the door if you're forgetful; look at your calendar to make sure you're mentally prepared for the day ahead)*
9:00 P.M. - *Chill*
10:00 P.M. - *Go to sleep*

*One load of laundry means: Wash it, dry it, fold it, put it in the right drawer, or hang it up (on a hanger). This should take 1.5 hours at the most.

NOTE: Sleep hygiene is an essential routine, even when you're young and seemingly full of life and energy and practically immortal. If you're getting enough restful sleep, you're less moody, your brain and heart function amazingly better, and you're much better equipped to navigate your waking hours. Your body must get a sound, deep sleep for your overall health, and it's vital to keeping weight in check. It's just as important as food and water!

John C. Maxwell said this, " You'll never change your life unless you change something you do daily. The secret to your success is found in your daily routine". Establishing a routine and some order in your life is an act of self-care and love. Creating a daily routine, that Jill is speaking of here is setting yourself up for success and is a key to optimal wellness.

A good routine sets the tone for our lives when we establish early how we are going to manage our time. Life can be unpredictable and a good routine will anchor us through some of those periods of uncertainty. It is great for our mental health to have certain rituals that we have established and don't have to think about. It is comforting to know you will be eating dinner at 6pm and that your head will hit the pillow by 10pm. A daily routine will helps reduce stress and contribute to your overall well-being. The earlier you establish a routine for yourself, the more peace of mind you have no matter what life throws at you.

CHRONOLOGICAL ORDER

Your Home and Your Space

So many new things are happening now! You have a career (or a job you love that's turning into a fantastic career). You may have found your soulmate! You've maybe even begun to have children and have the need to get a larger home. This, my friends, is when the accumulation starts. Bridal showers, baby showers, hand-me-downs of well-meaning relatives who give you antique and other types of furniture you don't like "for now" and yes, buying as much Pottery Barn and IKEA furniture as you can afford. Before you start pushing all the IKEA furniture into your 30s, here's some advice: If you're done using that furniture, and it has no real purpose in your home, please, for the love of all that's Danish furniture, let it go (and yes, I know EXACTLY how long it took you to assemble it, and I'm sorry).

Speaking of furniture, what do you need versus want? I get these questions a lot. The best example I can give you is when you walk into a hotel room, look around.

What's there?

- bed
- nightstand
- dresser
- chair
- lighting
- desk
- desk chair
- closet
- couch (varying sizes depending on room size)
- TV
- remote
- toilet
- sink
- linens for two people
- shower/tub
- tissues
- soap
- shampoo
- conditioner
- lotion

BONUS ITEMS:
mouthwash and a shower cap if you're lucky!

This list is what the hotels think you need for a few days. And if you think about it, you don't need much more than that in your home.

If you like to rehab furniture, or craft, or sew, or scrapbook, or just make stuff, make sure you have the space to store and work on said pieces of future art and unique creations.

Just like you don't want to build up debt, you will (probably) want to avoid building up possessions, especially if your space is already tight. Debt makes us feel overwhelmed because we don't have the funds to manage our bills and live life the way we want. Like debt, too much clutter around our living spaces makes us feel overwhelmed, and we run out of time to manage all of it and the room to enjoy our lives. The stuff becomes a full-time job to manage and to clean around, and who wants that? Nobody. Shopping is fun! But shopping means new stuff. And if you're like most people on this planet, you probably didn't get rid of the old stuff to make room for the new stuff. So please don't start the habit of buying a whole new wardrobe when your closets are stuffed. If you haven't worn out your appliances or you haven't taken the time to sell the ones you have, exactly why are you getting a new one right now? I know darn well that old perfectly good, albeit somewhat ugly and outdated in appearance, washing machine is going to sit in that basement for the next 30 years because:

"Maybe one of my friends wants it!" or
"I might need an extra washer if I have more kids," or
"My dad is going to come and get it and take it to some other guy when the weather gets better."

Umm...nope. No. No. You only need one washer in your house, unless, of course, you operate a laundromat. You might be wondering why I care so much about abandoned appliances in people's basements. Partly because those washers are amongst other rubble of misfit small and large appliances stored in people's basements that could have made another person who didn't care about stainless-steel fronts very happy and kept their clothes and dishes clean for decades!

Chronological Order

> The word "clutter" comes from the same root word as "clot". Webster's Dictionary defines it as "to run in disorder, to fill or cover with scattered or disordered things that impede movement or reduce effectiveness."
>
> The word "accumulate" is defined as "to gather or aquire an increasing number or quantity of." It is derived from the Latin words "cumulare" - to pile up, and "accumulare" - to heap together.

Once you decide to get rid of something, or you no longer use it, get rid of it right away, like immediately.

Accumulation begins when we run out of space and bring more items into that same area than there's room for. There can be a "creep" to this movement—a slow, subtle gliding motion of stuff coming in and NOTHING going out. It can take years to notice if the items are small. Be careful about this habit since you could turn around and be in your 80s and literally trip over your good intentions and big dreams. If you don't have space, see if you can rent studio space somewhere or book weekends away like scrapbookers do to devote the time, materials, and energy to achieve great results in a short, concentrated amount of time. I regularly encourage my clients to honor their creativity, and other than those two annoying limitations of time and space, you really can make that happen!

Paper and Information Organization
When it comes to organizing all that paper and information that comes and just sits there on an unsuspecting surface, here's some wisdom:

Create physical and digital matching files on your computer that have these four titles:

- To Pay
- To Call/Follow Up
- To Do
- To Buy Someday

Paper is a problem. I vividly recall a client who was very frustrated with her paper piles who pointed at them as soon as we walked into her home office. (Also known as the dining room table.) "Look at it!" She was pointing now. "It won't stop!"

Paper doesn't create piles on its own. It has to be carried, ignored, laid on a table, or placed on top of other papers.

What do you do with all of that paper? If you have existing paper, do this:

- Get a fine-tipped permanent marker
- Grab some Post-Its.
- If you don't have manila file folders, get a box of 50 at least.
- Find a timer of any kind.
- Go get a little box and write "Shred" on it.
- Get a paper bag and write "Recycle" on it.
- Write "Keep" on a Post-It. Place it on a clean, empty surface to the left-hand side. Put your "Shred" and "Recycle" boxes to the right of this "Keep" area.
- Set the timer for 30 minutes.

Begin sorting, using the OHIO technique (Only Handle It Once), and place those papers in the corresponding piles:

- Keep
- Shred
- Recycle

CHRONOLOGICAL ORDER

> Do you know what to shred? Check the IRS guidelines on shredding!

That's it. Keep going in 30 minute increments until all the paper has been decided upon. Take the recycling and dispose of it in the recycling bin that you always use, and if you have a large amount of shredding, take the bag to your local Staples or other office supply store that shreds for a low cost. Usually, you can get your shredding done for less than $1.00 per pound.

What do you shred? Once you've identified which information you don't need anymore you'll either be recycling it or shredding it if it has sensitive information. But how do you know what needs to be shredded? If your document has the following, you probably want to shred it:

- Date of Birth
- Social Security Number
- Account number of checking, investment, or savings accounts that are still active
- Group and Membership Numbers
- Credit Card Statements

Now, you might have a sizable keep pile. That's okay. Now we're going to sort it into action areas:

- To Pay
- To Call/Follow Up
- To Do
- To Buy Someday
- File
- To Shred

You'll want to create these areas using those manila files. If you want to be fancy-schmancy, use a label maker. If you want to hurry along, use that Sharpie and write these titles on each folder.

Now you'll be placing the paper into each of those folders, and you might be thinking, is that it? Is this the trick to getting my paper problem under control? Well... it's a start! Keep reading.

YOUR TWENTIES

Then you'll take your action folders (the top four) and put them where you can see them. You'll get your paper calendar or grab your cell phone or laptop if you use a digital calendar, and you're going to enter those action items.

To Pay: Set up a recurring reminder five days before the bill is due to pay the bill. If you trust your bank and don't want to forget a payment again, set up a recurring bill payment on your online banking website. Setting up a repeating payment through your banking service is typically safer than giving a company your information and letting them set up recurring payments for you!

To Call, To Do: Using the same calendar (please tell me you have one and don't have more than one calendar!), schedule your calls and tasks on the days you know you can deal with them. Please don't lump all the calls you have to make into tomorrow morning. It's not feasible, and you'll be setting yourself up for failure. You might be excited to finally have all these tasks in front of you, or you might feel overwhelmed. Just prioritize the three most important calls and errands and put those in for tomorrow. Put the rest into your calendar, spread out by importance and relevance to your schedule.

To Buy Someday: Oh, I like this one! This label phrase is a fantastic way to plan expenses in your budget! Instead of spending impulsively, this folder (and your bank balance) is at your fingertips and can be consulted before shopping. I love this folder. It's my dreaming folder, and every time I look at it, I'm reminded of the things I thought I wanted but never bought and how much money I saved in the process. I also notice that if one item (ad, a page from a catalog, etc.) remains in the folder, I probably still want it, and if I have the cash, I'll order it or go pick it up.

File: This might be boring, but it's essential. (Most boring stuff is.) Make sure you're putting the papers in the file folder only if you'll retrieve them again. Documents that are important to keep on file are:

- your vital records (see the later chapters of this book under "Life Essentials")
- financial documents like tax records, or where you're named as a mortgage holder, a stockholder, or have an investment portfolio original agreement of any kind
- legal documents, including marriage licenses, divorce decrees, or Power of Attorney records

CHRONOLOGICAL ORDER

To Shred: This category varies based upon your own privacy concerns, but there are general types of information that will need to be securely disposed of. Usually, sensitive information contains the following criterion:

- Social Security Numbers
- Dates of Birth
- Driver's License or State-Issued ID
- Passport Number
- Military ID

Other types of sensitive documents are:

- Legal documents such as completed divorces and custody agreements
- Expired warranties and insurance policies
- ATM Receipts
- Old checks (although keep in mind that when you give someone a check as payment, they also have your routing number and checking account number, so it seems like this may not be necessary – it's all up to you and your comfort level)
- Credit card bills or old credit card slips that show the entire number (yes, there are still companies that run a "credit card machine over a metal holder to take an imprint of the whole number...)
- Personal and emotional correspondence that you kept private and would like to stay in only your memory (in other words, these are bits of evidence of a part of your life that you do not want your loved ones to read after you die)

The method of shredding also depends on your comfort level. Some people are perfectly content with putting their sensitive documents in a box or bag and driving to an office supply place like Staples and handing it over to the clerk for disposal. Usually the clerk takes the box or bag, weighs it, then gives you the price based on the pounds shown on the scale display. Then the clerk takes the box and while behind the counter, feeds the papers from your box or bag into the slot in their locked receptacle, which is then picked up by an off-site document destruction company. For those individuals that are feeling very uncomfortable with the first scenario, there are on-site document destruction companies that will let you bring your documents to them to watch it get mulched to a pulp (which some people really enjoy doing!). These same companies will also send a shredding truck to your door. When the truck comes to your door, it's a good idea to have enough shredding bags or boxes to make it worth the cost for this service.

With less and less paper filing going on, you may want to set up digital files that EXACTLY match any paper file category titles so you remain consistent in your naming practices. Otherwise, you'll end up with your computer desktop screen looking a little like confetti on steroids.

How long do you keep records? Well, I'm not an accountant. But I can tell you that you can access all of what you need to keep on the IRS website. See? They're not all bad! Here's what they have to say about retention guidelines.

> *The length of time you should keep a document depends on the action, expense, or event which the document records. Generally, you must keep your records that support an item of income, deduction, or credit shown on your tax return until the period of limitations for that tax return runs out.*
>
> *The period of limitations is the timeframe in which you can amend your tax return to claim a credit or refund, or the IRS can assess additional tax. The information below reflects the periods of limitations that apply to income tax returns. Unless otherwise stated, the years refer to the period after the return was filed. Returns filed before the due date are treated as filed on the due date.*
>
> **Note:** *Keep copies of your filed tax returns. They help in preparing future tax returns and making computations if you file an amended return.*

Period of Limitations that apply to income tax returns

1. Keep records for three years if situations (4), (5), and (6) below do not apply to you.
2. Keep records for three years from the date you filed your original return or two years from the date you paid the tax, whichever is later if you file a claim for credit or refund after filing your return.

3. Keep records for seven years if you file a claim for a loss from worthless securities or bad debt deduction.
4. Keep records for six years if you don't report income that you should report, and it's more than 25% of the gross income shown on your return.
5. Keep records indefinitely if you don't file a return.
6. Keep records indefinitely if you file a fraudulent return.
7. Keep employment tax records for at least four years after the tax becomes due or is paid, whichever is later.

Apply the following question to each record as you decide whether to keep a document or throw it away.

Are the records connected to property?

Generally, keep records relating to property until the period of limitations expires for the year in which you dispose of the property. You must keep these records to figure out any depreciation, amortization, or depletion deduction and figure out the gain or loss when you sell or otherwise dispose of the property.

If you received property in a nontaxable exchange, your basis in that property is the same as the basis of the property you gave up, increased by any money you paid. You must keep the records on the old property and on the new property until the period of limitations expires for the year in which you dispose of the new property.

What should I do with my records for non-tax purposes?

> *When your records are no longer needed for tax purposes, don't discard them until you check to see if you have to keep them longer for other purposes. For example, your insurance company or creditors may require you to keep them longer than the IRS does.*

What about financial statements that make no sense? Can't I just drop them, envelope and all, into the folder? Suppose you get digital notifications or have created an online financial investment account with your advisor's company. In that case, it's very easy to ignore these messages and important information about YOUR money. Don't miss the emails and the letters, and just file them away. No, no, no. Open the envelope. Read them. If you aren't reading them because you don't understand them, please get an adviser, a parent, an accountant-friend—anyone who gets it—to help you. If you don't know anyone who can help, take a personal finance class. Most adult learning programs offer these very affordable classes at high schools and community colleges in their non-credit class curriculum.

Photographic Memories

What about the photos? Photos and memories take up a lot of room—on your phone, in your computer, and in my case, in boxes and bins. Are they organized? I mean, really organized? Does each photo have metadata? Metadata is the information that's important about the picture: the date, the subject, etc. If you want to find and use those photos again (let's say for an upcoming event where you need a slideshow or a photo album you want to make), you need to add metadata. Google Photos and Apple Photos will add some information for you, but the details and tagging are up to you!

Take some time to get to know your preferred way of saving, labeling, and organizing your photos. Are you able to find a photo when you need it, other than scrolling or swiping for a VERY LONG TIME? As pictures are taken, pick your favorites and save only those. Please don't keep the ones where there are closed eyes, blurry movements, or people you no longer like. These things won't change in this photo no matter what you do.

> Before you upload your pictures to any new cloud system:
>
> - Delete duplicates or photos you don't want to keep.
> - Make sure the information about the photo is correct. Changing metadata once the original images are uploaded usually isn't possible. Google Photos saves the metadata from the uploads, and this becomes the photo's date.
>
> Note: This pertains to photos you may have scanned in and are in a new folder, not the ones you've taken on your phone—those dates and information are saved and are accurate, even down to the location of the photo.
>
> When you're winding down your evening, or maybe you're a morning chiller, take five minutes to delete all the pictures you know you won't want or need later, like the meal you ate earlier today (that was beautiful, by the way) or the dress you weren't sure about three weeks ago and bought last week. You're on your phone looking at all sorts of stuff anyway before bed, so five more minutes won't seem like much.

Care about Your Home. This is also the time to get into great habits like a routine cleaning schedule and regular routines to maintain your home, vehicles, and any land around your home. Your older self will thank you. Here are some sample home-care habits that could work for you:

Daily:
- Wipe down surfaces—includes bathrooms and kitchen sinks. Keep some disinfectant wipes under your sink to make this easy, or keep a clean microfiber cloth that you only spray with water (we like Norwex cloths) to keep your surfaces clean.
- Check to see that your stovetop isn't disgusting. If you have gas burners, just dump the crumbs into the sink or the trash, and give it a quick wipe.
- Put your dirty clothes in the hamper to keep clothing clutter at bay, or hang up clothes you can wear again.
- Make sure your dishes, glasses, mugs, and silverware are clean and put away.

Weekly:
- Mop the floor (okay, you can Swiffer, just get it wet and make sure it's not sticky and gross).
- Vacuum the floor (sometimes I vacuum the floor, then mop it so that we don't have to sweep because I'm lazy about this).
- Clean out the fridge (get rid of that takeout that you had good intentions about).
- Clean the toilet bowls, all of them (this takes less than five minutes per toilet).
- Do some laundry.
- Take out the trash or the recycling if the bins are full. You'd be surprised at how many homes let the trash pile up. Trash only belongs in your home until the bag or can is full' then it needs to GO, GO, GO.
- Clean your tub. Do a good job—this is a major grime catcher, and it will only take you five minutes. Wear gloves if you're grossed out by soap slime. You'll get through this, I promise.

Monthly:
- Wipe out your oven.
- Clean your fridge and freezer shelves, throwing out the stuff you know darn well you won't make or eat.
- Clean your trash can and recycling bins (they're gross, even if you use a bag).
- If you have a garage, sweep it out.
- Check your batteries in your smoke detector and carbon dioxide detector.
- Clean your garbage disposal.
- Empty your dryer lint duct.

TIP: Buy and use just the essential cleaning supplies—watch how much of what you use so you can gauge how much you actually use. What are the essentials? Here you go:

Essentials:
- vinegar - diluted with water, this natural cleaner tackles windows, all other glass, and practically any surface in your home; also great for neutralizing carpet odors
- baking soda - besides being a natural deodorant, once it's mixed with water, it makes a powerful cleanser

- oil soap - for wood floors, wood furniture, and other surprising surfaces (read the label to be sure)
- dish soap - for more than just dishes! I love to use dish soap to get out stains in carpets since it's gentle
- cleaning cloths - use eco-friendly materials like Norwex brand cloths for glass and multi-purpose uses
- toothbrush - when your toothbrush gets replaced (every six months), use the old one for scrubbing in crevices, grout, around fixtures, and more little tight spaces
- bucket - for mopping, washing, and toting around your supplies in the house

Your Financial and Professional Goals

Financial Organizing 101

There seems to be a vast expanse of life years ahead of you, and you're more than just a little bit confident that you have plenty of time to make decisions. You're right! Lots of time. For me, it was lots of time to worry about my future. I wasn't going to do it at 24—or 28, for that matter. I just wanted to make sure the bottles were full and warm for the babies, the diapers were changed, the laundry was done, and the meals were cooked and cleaned up. Sleep and planning were two activities that escaped me on a daily basis. I remember going to work for the first time since I had the kids and leaving behind a screaming three-year-old who didn't know where the hell she was or why a stranger was holding her. I remember not realizing that Barney music was playing the entire way to work until I found myself singing "Kookaburra" quietly under my breath. I walked into the administrative office that morning with bleary eyes and a guilty heart, and in the process of onboarding, I was filling forms about a retirement account. What? I was only 28! I was just reentering the workforce—retirement was as far away as it could possibly be. Retirement was for older people, not me!

You may be hopping from apartment to apartment or going from renting to buying. Things change dramatically in your financial world when you buy a home. Accountability goes way up, along with risk. The mortgage payment is nothing to mess around with, and neither are those student loans.

Lenders get very salty when they're not paid or not paid on time, and take it from me if you miss one payment, your credit score is affected for a long period of time. That, in turn, affects your ability to borrow for that car or get another loan of any kind. If you wanted to apply for that Master's program and needed to borrow, your chances of getting approved or getting a low-interest rate (that you won't see paid off until you're in your 30s) are pretty slim.

Please, please, please track your spending!!! This is easier and easier to do now with apps and our phones. Banks offer insights for expense tracking so you can budget more wisely. I think when we hear the word "budget" we think of limits. Yes, this is true. But what's more empowering is to think of a budget as how you can live within your means AND have the life you want to do the things you enjoy. (Note: I didn't say HAVE the things you enjoy.)

J The year was 1987. I was a 17-year-old fresh-faced freshman at Villanova University, going to study Political Science and then become a lawyer. I was so excited to even BE there. The fact that I got in was miraculous enough, but it was a family legacy steeped in generational tradition for me to go there. When I was born, my father clothed me in Villanova baby and toddler outfits, while my mother helplessly rolled her eyes and watched him parade around his future Villanova grad. I was the only female in the family who was a student there. My dad, my uncles, my cousins—all proud and accomplished Villanova alumni. (No pressure.) I vividly remember excitedly going to the campus bookstore to get the textbooks I needed for my first semester and was blown away by the cost of the books alone. I needed the books, so that was a mandatory expense. I liked the price of the used books and prayed that whoever had it before me and had highlighted and underlined copiously was actually smart. To even get to the book part of the bookstore, I had to wade through the many aisles and racks of school merchandise first. What a rookie I was! I might as well have tried to just buy milk at Target.

There it all was, gleaming at me wantonly—Villanova University ball caps, sweatshirts (in my size!), t-shirts, scarves, keychains, and mugs! All I wanted was a sweatshirt, but it was $35. After buying the books, I had maybe that much left in my checking account at the time since I was living paycheck to paycheck. I was a banquet waitress on the weekends, and I worked at a township golf course and JCPenney during the week. I took care of and lived with my grandmother in her tiny house in Norristown, and we always seemed to be struggling to pay the bills.

I drove a beat-up, rusty, tomato-red Toyota Celica with the duct tape endeavoring to keep the bottom of the car together. Friends of mine called this the "Flintstone-mobile" because of the holes and because we knew there would be a time when we would probably have to use our feet through those holes to power the car. (I sort of miss that little beast of a vehicle.) So, when the attractive young man (wearing the exact sweatshirt I wanted) at the Discover Card vendor table in that crowded bookstore asked me if I would like to sign up for a low-interest credit card to buy what I needed for school, I grabbed a pen. Well, two thousand dollars and three years later, I was officially in debt over my head. If you've ever been hungry going into a grocery store on a busy Sunday and been sweetly asked to buy Thin Mints by a seven-year-old cute Girl Scout, you may be able to understand what happened to me that day. It wasn't until many years later, and I mean when I was 28, that I finally paid off the final sum of $3,500. That $2,000 was all I'd spent on what I "needed" during college, but that additional $1,500 was my interest charges. That's what happens when you don't pay off your credit card every month. I remember trying to apply for a credit card to pay for my wedding dress in 1993, and I was rejected, all because I had been late twice on a Discover Card payment years before. My fiancé had to buy my gown, which was only $350. (I bought the shoes and veil, which came to $100. And yes, that stressed me out, too.)

Oh, by the way, I did graduate from Villanova on time ("Miracles happen every day!" my father used to say). I didn't become an attorney, much to my parents' chagrin. I became a poorly paid but happy case manager at a community mental health center in Norristown. Career choices can adversely or favorably affect your bottom line, so if you didn't play the Game of Life as a kid, you're playing it now, for real. It's hard to choose what will be emotionally and financially fulfilling when you're young.

YOUR TWENTIES

 Okay, Jill, I need to interrupt here. I must chime in and pray these really smart 20-somethings who are so wise even to purchase this book will really hear what I have to say here.

THIS IS THE TIME to learn how to manage and respect money!! Trust me, you don't want to be me at the age of 50 going for the first time to visit with a financial planner...and if you are me...well, kudos to you too for having the courage to face the fact that you totally blew the whole "financial management" piece in your life up until this point. Learn how to live within your means! You don't want to be stuck in the loop of paying high interest rates and taking years to pay down the debt of items you now wonder why the heck you ever bought in the first place. Make it a priority and learn how to create a simple budget. Don't put off these vital steps when you're in your 20s that will set you up for success when you reach your 50s and beyond! Jill is right!! Don't go and sign up for the Discover Card your first day on campus, buying into the lie that you NEED it just in case of an emergency...because guess what? When the Travis Scott concert rolls onto campus during Spring Fling, you ARE GOING to whip out that credit card and charge that ticket and lie to yourself about how you're going to pay it back in full the next $75.00 paycheck you get from your work-study job on campus. Don't do it!

You won't pay it back—in fact you'll be charging away for those vente pumpkin lattes, pizzas, and beer! Within six months, you'll have maxed out that card and probably will be on your way to charging up another card! DON'T DO IT! Run far away from that sign-up table! Burn every one of those offers that start tempting you to get another credit card! This is the "crack" of your financial future! Just say NO! Resist the devil. PAY CASH and learn now how to save for what you most want. Trust us here, and you'll build not only your net worth but also your self-worth!

If you've already created the monster of debt, my advice is to start with the truth! Where are you spending your money each day? What are you doing with the money you have? To be a better steward of your resources, it's best to first start by tracking your spending for a few weeks. Be sure to check with your financial institution; many banks offer spending trackers and alerts to remind you of your set spending limit. There are apps available to help you as well. Check out the Wally app! It will help you track your spending.

I found this to be a vital step for me to better understand my spending habits. It was quite an eye-opener, and I was able to see the holes in my dam! There were holes I needed to plug if I was going to be able to afford some of the items on my bucket list. I now had an honest overview of my spending habits and was able to create a budget. I then could shift some of the money I was spending on cable TV and double espressos and funnel toward things that were vital to my reaching my goals. I now had a clearer picture, and acknowledging my true spending habits, I then could take steps toward change and make a budget that fit my needs. There's an app for that, too, if this seems overwhelming for you to do on your own. Check out www.youneedabudget.com. The app was great, but what I found to be the best was facing it all head-on by setting an appointment with a financial planner. I kept putting off making this appointment because I was wrapped up in so much fear and quite frankly embarrassed by the amount of debt and lack of resources in my life at the time approaching age 50…but facing this fear head-on became one of the greatest lessons of my life. My financial planner didn't make me feel horrible; she made me feel empowered and hopeful for a brighter future. She helped me make a step-by-step strategic plan to manage my debt and begin saving for what was most important to me. I left wishing I had met with her when I was 20 because if I had, I probably would have already checked some of those items off my bucket list by now and would be debt-free!

Let's talk about adulting at work a little, shall we?

If you're currently employed in your first "real job" you're now learning how to manage your day at work and the expectations of your boss and coworkers. This is no easy task! Remember that most jobs take about three to six months for you to feel like you're "getting it." I was so hard on myself in my first job because I thought I should know everything right away about how things worked there, who was who, what was what, etc. It takes time to get to know everything expected of us in our roles and find out how to be a successful part of the company's culture. Be patient with yourself. Stress and anxiety can wreak havoc on your health and relationships. Just because we live in a world that revolves around instant, well, *everything*, doesn't mean that you personally need to assimilate to every new ability immediately. You are a human, after all, not a robot.

Ah, yes, your first "real job." Mine was as a manager of a furniture store. I had just graduated from college and had a degree in Interior Design. At the time, I had zero confidence in myself to set off and start my own business as an interior designer. I let fear stop me from pursuing that dream. (Don't do this! All things are possible if you believe!) But I had enough confidence to sell the crap out of furniture and was able to use my design skills to help others pick out the perfect pieces for their homes. I genuinely loved the work. I quickly started noticing areas where I could improve the furniture showroom layout and realized there was no onboarding process for training new hires. I began sharing my ideas with the VP of the company. My showroom was outselling the other nine showrooms we had in Manhattan, and the higher ups started to take notice. Before long, I wrote the company training manual for new employees and got promoted to district manager. When I heard the company chatter that they were thinking of expanding into other cities, I let it be known that I was open to moving and would love to help in any way I could. A few months later, I was packed up and moving to Boston, locating a new showroom space and setting up shop! I had become a vital part of the company. This all came to pass because I consistently treated this company as if it were my own. I loved the customers, the other employees, and offered to learn about others' job responsibilities. I led by example, and there was no job I was unwilling to do if needed. I once even helped unload an 18-wheeler filled with furniture because the truck came unexpectedly, and we didn't have our stock crew available. When you constantly look for ways to bless others, you'll be noticed. It's unlikely you'll get fired from a job if you have this attitude. Just like the Boy Scouts say: DO YOUR BEST!!

Fear is a liar! Tell it to shut up; you can do anything you set your mind to!

J   Not to diffuse this reality check, but if you have physical limitations (like being 5 feet tall like me, who may never play center on a professional basketball team) or talents that are better off being hobbies (like I'm a violinist who will just stick to playing Beethoven's symphonies at home), it's okay to create and manifest new dreams. These new goals might push you past the usual fears you might be experiencing. Trepidation is one thing, but actual anxiety is another roadblock entirely.

Fear is one of our biggest limitations. Unfortunately, it stops us from moving forward on our goals, but sometimes it can be prohibitive to a healthy mind. If you have real anxiety, and I mean the kind where your chest gets tight and your heart races in stressful situations, it's time to address that. A lifetime of being afraid is no way to live. Talking to someone about what worries you is a beginning, and there are many treatments for Anxiety Disorder that can make your present and your wonderful future not only more bearable but surprisingly enjoyable.

Your Relationships and Social Life

J   People who age successfully have made sure that they keep connected to those they care about most and have made time to enjoy hobbies and activities they love as an individual. Healthy relationships value this and encourage our partners to enjoy time apart. It's okay to spend a weekend fishing, enjoy a sporting event together, or have a spa day with your best friend. It's also necessary to have some friends or couples your age, but also some older couples who can bring wisdom and perspective into your lives. You're going to need this! Establish this early in your relationships and respect and honor each other's interests. Be proactive in encouraging this in your mate, and make sure you're both maintaining and nurturing vital connections. Resentment builds when the balance between "me" time and "couple" time is leaning too heavily in one direction.

YOUR TWENTIES

If you're single, be careful not to go overboard on going out all the time. This is where many find they're overindulging on too much beer and wine, not sleeping right, and wasting way too much money. Learn self-control, self-care, and the value of alone time. Take time to sit with yourself and spend time daydreaming, reflecting, and planning for all that brings just you joy! I like to schedule a few days a month where I have nothing planned. I let the day unfold as it happens. I never even leave my bed some of those days. I sleep, watch old movies, or read a good book. Other days I spontaneously jump in my car and spend the day at a museum or go for a long drive out into the country. These are days that change up my routine and allow me just to be me! No agenda, no expectations. I've learned they're vital, and if I could go back in time and tell my 20- something self this advice, I would. The pace I was trying to keep up with when I was in my early 20s resulted in several trips to the ER with panic attacks. It was my first life lesson that I wasn't invincible, and I needed to learn how to allow my body and mind to rest.

What I learned most about in my 20s was "me." I discovered who I was, what made me tick, what scared the crap out of me, what I was good at, what I sucked at, what I wanted to learn, and what I would make sure I got to do. One day somewhere in this decade, I discovered ME, and I was going to be okay! I was no longer looking at others around me—I was now looking at who I was becoming. It's in your 20s that you really do get introduced to yourself. So, make sure you spend time uncovering who you are, and the earlier you learn to love yourself, the better!

Let's say that you finally figure all this out: the meals, the housework, the job, the routines, the dog walks—all of it. You're on TOP! Getting a paycheck, buying new clothes from a genuine department store (although NOTHING is wrong with Goodwill shopping), and making sure all your bills are paid. You have so much autonomy and freedom to do whatever the heck you want, when you want, and life is good! Then, you meet someone, fall madly in love, and decide to get married or move in together. This is when it gets interesting!

Here is a potential scenario that might sound familiar:

"Oh! Are you going out? I thought we would sit on the couch tonight, cuddle, and watch Hallmark/Star Wars/ (fill in the blank)!"

33

Chronological Order

"Oh! Okay, that's okay. I was just going to go have a drink with (friend since childhood)."

"Oh! Okay, that's okay! I can order some takeout and watch this movie on my own. Go have fun."

You ask yourself: "*Is this a trap?*"

Maybe it is, or perhaps the person you're living with or married to is being genuine. I bet you anything they just want to be with you. And there will be times you just want to be with them, and they're preoccupied or have plans you forgot about. This is where understanding and love come in. The understanding part is not jumping to the worst conclusion: "Obviously he/she doesn't love me and prefers to be without me." The opposite is usually true: "He/she loves me and wants to spend time with me but also has important people in his/her life, too." The love part is where you agree that love is not envy, mistrust, or selfishness. If you believe you can allow the other person in your life to live their best life, even if that means some nights you aren't there, then you're setting the path for a VERY healthy relationship. How do I know this? Because I took it waaaaaay too personally when a husband or boyfriend (I didn't have both at the same time, so stop it!) went somewhere without me, and it caused LOTS of problems. When I got older and developed more of my own interests, this lessened, the insecurities fell away, and when someone did this to me (questioned why I was going out, why I was taking this friend here or there, etc.) I wasn't happy and felt cornered, not trusted, and NOT loved.

THIS IS THE MOMENT; this is the moment right now. You get to decide to go ahead with your plans out and about or stay home. Is it caving? Is it giving in to guilt? This is entirely your decision. However, you have to be careful here because when you stop doing what you like doing and being with friends you've always enjoyed being with in order to please your partner, you're in trouble. If you start bargaining away who you are day by day and week by week, I promise you that you'll wake up in your 40s or 50s and wonder where "you" went. Be careful to learn how to compromise with your partner so you can share new experiences with them and retain some of the activities that define who you are and what you enjoy.

Couples need time apart. Healthy relationships respect and honor each other's individual interests and encourage you to maintain friendships.

Part of me developing my identity was developing friendships outside of high school and college. Some of the best friends I've had were from my first "real" job after graduating. Don't get me wrong, I loved working at restaurants and JCPenney because it was easy and fun, but the real challenges, and subsequent genuine relationships with my coworkers, were established in that first career setting.

Speaking of friendships at work, I must say that I was glad the happy hour was invented before I started my career. If it wasn't, I think my coworkers and I would have put a patent on that reasonably quickly. It was a vital way to blow off steam and truly vent about our day. The field of social work was very stressful and riddled with pressure, emotions, and anxiety about our clients and their complex situations. We were exposed to some pretty awful and traumatic situations and events in those young years. I was almost killed in a drive-by shooting while eight months pregnant with my son, just because I'd decided to walk to my client's home instead of drive. (In my defense, it was a nice day, and I thought it was silly to take a car to a house that was just two blocks from our office.) We operated without cell phones, got chased down alleys, were stalked a time or two, and were followed into tunnels at the state hospital by people who were definitely in the mood to hurt us. We were threatened, lied to, and berated by our clients. Granted, these people we served were mentally ill, but it was still disconcerting, no matter how many grains

> of salt you added to the situation. My fellow case managers were very levelheaded and knew how to redirect the angriest and most intoxicated of clients. Still, even the strongest resolve can crack when you're overloaded with a caseload of complicated and challenging people to help. We would poke our heads into each other's offices during a particularly stressful day, and all we had to say was "'Casa Maria."
>
> We all knew where this lovely Mexican oasis was and when to report. We ate chips and salsa, had a margarita or a beer (or both), and told our stories of the day. Our group was large, and we would take over the place. It was a quick impromptu party, but it was important for our mental health.

Work/life balance is a bit of a misnomer. That phrase has good intentions. It does. But I would prefer something else, like "make time for your priorities," but it's not as catchy. If you want a sneak peek into how to define what the important stuff is, and you can't wait to make it to your 30s to learn this, I encourage you to read ahead.

The formula is simple, but the follow-through can be complicated and takes some effort:

Stress = Actions vs. Priorities

Peace = Actions + Priorities

About Your Parents (and Grandparents)
If you're in your 20s, your parents are most likely in their 40s or 50s. To understand them a little more than you already think you do, we encourage you to read those chapters of the book, particularly the Identity and Relationships segments. We're all coping with different aspects of aging, yes, even at your age. Despite what your life looks like now, it's crucial to understand what your parents and stepparents (if applicable) are experiencing emotionally, financially, and physically and what you need to be planning for down the road. In your 20s, these guardians of your life are still guiding you. They're still

helping you make emotional and financial decisions, and if you're getting married for the first time, they're possibly involved in helping you pull that together, whether you like it or not. (Hopefully, you like it!) If you're in your young 20s, maybe they're helping you to transition out of college and into a career by putting a roof over your head, feeding you, and taking you shopping for your interview suit or dress. Maybe they're working out your budget with you or helping you plan your next adventure in life. Remember, they have about 20 years on you—use that good knowledge and experience!

I know everyone tells you this, and sometimes you might roll your eyes in response, but please thank them, either in writing or by giving them a kind word. As much as I hate to admit it, some parents are easier to thank than others. It all depends on your relationship with your parents and stepparents, of course, but a little expression of gratitude goes a long way.

If you're lucky enough to have living grandparents and even more fortunate to have a relationship with them, spend some time with them. Get their stories and wisdom and share some of yours. Many older people get so much energy from younger people, and younger people are a lot more fulfilled than they let on after spending quality time with their grandparents. You can improve their lives, too, with everything from shopping for them, cleaning their homes, running little errands, lending a hand with baking for the holidays, or trimming the hedges in their yard. You can set up new technology for them and teach them how to use it! You have many gifts you can give them in return for all of the unconditional love you've received from them.

Now, if your parents and grandparents aren't helpful to you, or you don't have a good relationship with them, it's okay to seek guidance from aunts, uncles, cousins, or anyone who has and can act as a great mentor for you. Sometimes it's an older coworker who has time to spare (maybe they don't have a close family, either). It could be someone from a group or club you're in with whom you identify. You don't have to go it alone—someone will always want to help you. Like Mr. Rogers said, "Look for the helpers. You will always find people who are helping."

Life Essentials

The following list is what we call the Life Essentials, the must-dos! These are the items that, as professionals, we see over and over again not being taken care of! They're the essential items that must be done but sadly are put off, never talked about, or avoided. They're matters that seem to be assumed everyone has taken care of, but in all honesty, they're more frequently never done, or if they are done, they're outdated, never reviewed, and often misplaced! We'll mention these throughout the decades and fully educate you on why you must have them! Throughout this book, you'll learn more about each item on this list. The whole point of this book is to help you live your best life as you age. You must take care of these issues, and we'll shed light as to why!

Don't forget! Make sure you have the following elements in place (yes, even in your 20s!) before moving on to your next decade:

- Life Insurance (see Life Essentials Chapter)
- Wills (see Life Essentials Chapter)
- Living Will
- Vital Records
- Power of Attorney
- Home Inventory
- Health Benefits
- Care and Living Plan

You will see this list at the end of every chapter, as a gentle reminder of what you should have accomplished at the end of that decade of living. A more detailed description of each Life Essential can be found at the end of this book.

YOUR THIRTIES

Your Identity and Well-being

> "Life moves pretty fast. If you don't stop and look around once in a while, you could miss it" - Ferris Bueller, *Ferris Bueller's Day Off*

Time goes by quickly (I know, "duh").

Your 30s might just become your favorite decade of living if you let it. It sure is the most accelerated part of your life, in my humble opinion. This decade just zooms past with such fun escapades as marriage, parenthood, home ownership, working longer hours to rise within your career path and pay off school loans, and upgrades to just about every area of your life. No wonder you might miss such marvelous experiences as rocketing personal growth, appreciating your family, or how your friends are really doing outside of the social media atmosphere.

It's time for you to slow down! You may now find that life, this adulting, is feeling a bit overwhelming. You may have taken the giant leap into marriage by now, having purchased your first home, and suddenly your name has been changed to Mommy or Daddy. You may be pushing hard to move up the company ladder and wonder if you even love the work you're doing.

Life is swirling at a breakneck pace in your 30s, and it's time to take stock of what matters most in your life. You may think you need to work harder so you can have that granite countertop or get that fancy gas-guzzling SUV...but count the cost. Do you want to be a slave to the expense of the stuff, or do you want to be able to spend time at Junior's baseball game? What's most important to you? You need to be thinking about this because the reality is unless you have clear boundaries, you'll never have peace, especially when your boss rolls his eyes when you request the vacation time you're entitled to. It's time to step back and evaluate what matters most to you and this growing family you created.

I would say I spent most of my 30s STRESSED OUT! In the chaos of life, I began the cycle of neglecting myself and shelved many of the dreams I once had. Stop. Don't let this happen to you. It's vital for you to learn how to manage it all and prioritize what matters most to you and your family. Stress is one of the most significant factors in the acceleration of disease. You need to make your health and well-being a priority now while you're young enough to create healthy habits and set a good example for your children, if you have them.

Allow me to be real here. I haven't taken care of my body. I spent years stressed, depressed, inactive, and filling my face with Nutty Bars from Little Debbie. I'm now in my 50s, 100 pounds overweight, and have spent what has felt like a lifetime on the yoyo diet craze. We're blessed today to have knowledge at our fingertips. We can easily spend time learning about how our bodies function and what they need to thrive at any time we choose. I'm on my own pursuit to get my health in order so I can fully enjoy the experiences I plan to have. I'm now learning how to break a lifetime of bad habits. I'm also discovering that I enjoy exercising, which was a big surprise to me because I spoke about how much I hated exercise for years. It truly was a lie I was telling myself. So, as we're writing this book, I'm pursuing transforming my life and health as I get older.

Your body was designed to heal itself.

People who are thriving through their 80s and beyond are people who have learned this lesson and took the steps needed to stay healthy. They make wise food choices, make time for themselves and their children, keep their bodies in motion, and let go of whatever doesn't give them joy! It's time for you to let go of that which weighs you down. Your future self will thank you for it! It's truly much easier to make these changes in your 30s than when you reach your 50s like me.

In my pursuit and study to age well, I came across the book, *The Blue Zones: Lessons for Living Longer from the People Who've Lived the Longest* by Dan Buettner. Dan has uncovered longevity communities around the world where a high population of the people are living beyond the age of 100. They call these the Blue Zones. I find it pretty amazing that even though the Blue Zones are often from opposite corners of the world and have different religions and languages, they all have similar habits that enable them to live long, full, rich lives.

Here are the nine commonalities Dan Buettner has discovered to their longevity:

- You've got to move! Walk, hike, dance, bike, garden... keep moving!
- Add seven years to your life by having a sense of purpose!
- Schedule downtime daily—walk, pray, nap, go to happy hour!
- The 80% rule: People in the Blue Zones don't eat until they're 100% full. The 20% gap could be why they're not obese. They also eat their smallest meal in the late afternoon and early evening and don't eat anything after that.
- Eat your beans: Fava, black, soy, and lentils are the cornerstone of most centenarian diets.
- Enjoy one or two glasses of wine each day with friends and a meal! The key here is not to drink alone.
- Belong to a faith-based community. Regular attendance can add four to 14 years to your life.
- Family first! This means keeping aging parents and grandparents nearby or in the home (it lowers disease and mortality rates of children in the home, too). They commit to a life partner (which can add up to three years of life expectancy) and invest in their children with time and love (they'll be more likely to care for you when the time comes).
- Right tribe: The world's longest-lived people chose—or were born into—social circles that supported healthy behaviors. Okinawans created "moais" which are groups of five friends who committed to each other for life. I love this!!

I would encourage you to do your own research and start incorporating these habits into your life now. Your older self will thank you for it! To learn more about the Blue Zones, visit their website, BlueZones.com.

Your Home and Your Space

Life is in full swing! Your career is accelerating, and you're growing in so many ways—developing more friendships due to working, parenting, and your neighborhood or apartment community. You're socializing in a whole different way than you did in your 20s, and the core groups of friends you have usually have a lot in common with you. Whether you're single or married, you are BUSY. You're creating a real home now, not just piecing things together. You're developing your own sense of style and possibly seeing that the beer pong table might be better suited for someone else's back deck. There's usually a lot of pressure to have the best furniture from the on-trend stores at this age.

There was a huge trend back when I was in my early 30s to have a PLAID couch. It was so popular! EVERYONE HAD ONE. I had shopped around and finally found one I thought I could afford. It was indeed comfortable and totally cool. I finally fit in!

Yes! When people came over, I was proud that I had a couch just like everyone else. It was a roomy, cushion-laden, green-and-red-and-white plaid number with soft arms, a blanket, and a couple of hunter green throw pillows for accent. The kids climbed up on it year after year for TV watching, book reading, and general cuddling. It was great until it wasn't. I suddenly felt odd a few years later to have this loud couch in the middle of my living room. I couldn't wait to replace it with something else! I hated it! Why did I think this huge monstrosity was the end-all, be-all of my home? BECAUSE EVERYONE ELSE DID, TOO. I wanted so desperately to have something new and almost broke the bank because of it. I remember the kids wanted a Little Tikes outdoor playset, and because I spent so much buying the couch, I didn't have the money. They ended up climbing and playing on the sofa, so it was sort of the same, right? After the lovely behemoth of a sofa had run its course, I gave it to a friend's friend who "just needed a couch" and then took a hand-me-down Ethan Allen set from my mother, which ended up lasting me another few years until we moved again.

CHRONOLOGICAL ORDER

Your 30s are a perfect time to invest in the structural and maintenance aspects of your home, if you own a home, and keep your environment clean, to avoid two concerns:

- a neglected house
- a dirty house

Having a good routine that you've carried forward from your 20s is so important. It will be a lifetime habit that will make life easier in whatever home you choose from now until the end of your life.

Shopping is fun, but shopping can be bad.

For years we've been using shopping as a reason to:

- get out of the house more (Amazon has reversed this necessity overall, but ... Target!)
- build up what we need for our homes like furniture, lighting, accessories, and appliances.
- purchase gifts for our loved ones and friends (and even people we don't like but feel obligated to buy a gift for).
- make sure holidays aren't a catastrophic disappointment for our entire family, but especially the kids.
- pair with a lunchtime excursion with a good friend for socialization (drinking wine or any form of alcohol at lunch can increase your desire to buy things you don't need or want).
- take a little break from our spouses and significant others (let's be honest, we've all done it).
- cheer ourselves up, AKA as "retail therapy," AKA fill a void.

So, if I had to ask you which one of these six reasons contributes the most unnecessary household accumulations, which would you choose?

What? You bought something purely to make you feel better about your life, your home, yourself?? Completely normal. People do this all the time. I've done it. I regret it only later if it was:

- too expensive
- too small

- ugly when I got it home
- the person I gave it to believes it has elements of all the above

And since I'm a professional organizer, I have to remind everyone reading this that when this becomes a real problem, you begin to see crowding of existing spaces. We might see clothing stacked on the floor around the perimeter of the room, on top of the dresser, under the dresser, or on chairs. This is due to no longer having room in dresser drawers or on shelves. In extreme situations, the clothes and other articles are actually in bed with their owners. Here are some clothing storage capacity guidelines:

- 1 tall dresser (holds about 60 articles of clothing for an average-sized person)
- 1 bureau or chest of drawers (holds approximately 40-60 articles of clothing)
- 1 closet with four linear feet of hanging space, with accompanying four linear feet of shelving above or below (holds about 50 hanging garments and depending on ceiling height, it can contain 15 to 40 folded pieces of clothing)
- 1 under bed storage bin (holds about 10 pairs of shoes) for off-season shoes and boots
- 2 nightstands for bedside lighting, books, chargers, pens, notebooks, and personal items

Organizing your bedroom closet can be VERY rewarding, assigning a place for each pair of shoes, sweatshirts, pairs of jeans, etc. Organizing supplies are fun to buy, but you can go overboard if you don't match the organizer to the amount of or type of clothing or accessory you're trying to store.

A few of my favorite organizing goodies are:

- thin velvet hangers to save space for hanging clothes
- a hanging shoe organizer—it holds all sorts of things other than shoes!
- clear stackable square bins for folded clothing
- an easy-to-fill and easy-to-grab laundry basket
- shelf dividers to keep folded clothing from toppling over
- a shoe rack for the floor to store shoes you wear frequently
- a popped-up paper grocery bag or small cardboard box for items you no longer want or need (These items can go to donation centers or consignment stores when the bag or box is full.)

Remember, if it doesn't fit in your closet or in the furniture you own, you probably have too much! All the cute organizing supplies in the world won't make too many clothes fit.

Take inventory of the stuff you need all the time. I call them "never-outs":

- lightbulbs
- trash bags
- batteries
- paper products (toilet paper, paper towels)
- detergent (laundry, dish)
- soap
- shampoo/conditioner

The list goes on and on, but every time you see yourself getting low on these items, you can add them to your favorite shopping cart like Amazon, and when you're ready to check out, they're all there. You can even start "subscribing" to these items online, and unless you stop the service, you'll receive your "never-outs" once a month. Our local grocery store does the same thing with my account. You can have your standard lists ready to go, and when you need to add to them, it asks if this is an item to "add to my list" or not. I absolutely love this feature since I seem to buy the same things over and over again, and I don't have to go hunting for them each time I go online.

What if you have more than daily or weekly clutter? What if the stuff has become a problem?

Here are my top ten do's and don'ts when it comes to your stuff:

10 Clutter DO's

1. Work when your energy is good, and put some music on (if you like music; if you hate to listen to music, do NOT put music on).
2. Get help: Call a professional organizer, a good friend, or a family member. It forces you to focus and to make decisions you wouldn't typically make.

YOUR THIRTIES

Make sure the person you choose to help you is nonjudgmental. This is KEY. *The person you choose should care about you and not use shame, scary facial expressions, or influence to make you get rid of objects you're using and enjoying. A relative who will remain nameless (she knows who she is!) once tried to have me get rid of a drinking glass I had just put on the counter in my kitchen. It still had water in it! This person isn't the person you want to help you.*

3. Set the timer—have a beginning and an end to your decluttering! Do you have a timer on your cell phone? That can be a good and bad thing. Why is it good? It's handy! Why is it bad? Because that's where your biggest distractions sit! So, use the oven timer, an egg timer, or The Time Timer.
4. Set up bins and receptacles—Keep, Garbage, Donate, Sell, Not Sure.
5. Work on one area or room at a time. Set things near the door that need to go somewhere else, and take them there only after you're finished organizing the space you're in.
6. Work left to right, "reading the room," then top to bottom (see "Read that Room like a Book" in the Fifties chapter).
7. Use the OHIO technique—Only Handle It Once, meaning you have to decide about that item's storage location (even if it's the shredder) as soon as you touch it, no exceptions. (This technique is described in much more detail in the next chapter, "Your Forties")
8. Determine the need, frequency, and value of each item.
9. Contain and label everything you possibly can so every item has a home (e.g., "Hair Stuff").
10. Make ONE more pass through your Keep items before you're done, and monthly FOR THE REST OF YOUR LIFE!

Chronological Order

Monthly, look around your home.

Review the clothes, shoes, and accessories in your closet. Are they currently things you enjoy wearing or look good on you? If not, so many people need clothing, shoes, coats, and belts, so please give them the dignity to buy what they need at a local charitable thrift shop.

Check the back of your junk drawer for items you no longer reach for. Do you still need them? Once I found a broken Christmas ornament I'd intended to fix. I finally threw it away, as it was in the back of the drawer. If I had wanted it, honestly, I would have fixed it right away. Once you tuck something in a drawer, it's really easy to forget about it. Once you forget about it and all the other stuff you tucked away, your junk drawer truly isn't about batteries, matches, scissors, tape, stamps, and pens anymore. It's a bunch of ACTUAL JUNK.

Clean out your car and get it ready for the next 30 days. It's so easy to neglect your car, but unless you live in a city where you ride a train or bus to work every day, you're IN YOUR CAR a lot. If you're a parent, and your kid has to go to school, sports practice, or meet up with friends, there's stuff in your car that you didn't bring in: Spilled juice, cracker crumbs, a souvenir cup from Disney on Ice, boogers (that's right, I said boogers), and dirt. It becomes a stinky, sticky closet reflecting a lot of use and good intentions. Remove obvious trash and anything you meant to bring into your home but weren't able to. Check under the seats—you might find money! Vacuum it. Wipe it down. Seriously, if you do this once a month, you won't dread it when you go to do it after a year or more. Keep a big bag or a small box in your car. ALL THE TIME. This way, your hands, which are already full, can handle carrying everything into your home in ONE trip. That's what we try to do with the 14 grocery bags anyway, right?

10 Clutter DON'Ts

1. Don't organize when you're tired or hungry!
2. Try not to tackle big jobs (attic, garage) alone.

3. Don't buy any new items (except food) until you're finished with your organizing project.
4. Don't allow interruptions—phone calls, texts, emails—to distract you. Turn off your phone notifications or turn off the sound altogether.
5. Don't criticize yourself for having "so much stuff," just keep moving and be proud that you're doing something about it NOW.
6. Don't worry about not knowing how to organize—it's a skill, and it CAN be learned!
7. Don't think that because something is old, it can't be used by someone else—donate it.
8. Don't run around the house giving items a new home once you have them in your hand—this will only distract you from the space you were in.
9. Don't put stuff in the attic or basement "for now"—they'll be forgotten about, and they might get ruined by water or pests.
10. Don't hesitate to ask for professional help if you can't stop hoarding and collecting things out of fear.

It's essential for you to know the difference between normal accumulating vs. collecting due to hoarding disorder. *Normal accumulations usually occur due to too much spending, lack of impulse control, or time-and-space-management challenges. Hoarding disorder is a brain-based disorder that usually results from one or more traumatic incidents and causes attachment to objects, or animals, often affecting the person's quality of life significantly. "Difficulty to discard" even one of the many possessions in the home is often one of the indications that clinical intervention is required. It's imperative* **to not cause harm to someone with hoarding disorder by removing items forcefully or without their knowledge and permission.**

> *The Institute of Challenging Disorganization® defines chronic disorganization (CD) as "disorganization that persists over a long period of time, frequently undermines quality of life, and recurs despite repeated self-help attempts. Chronic disorganization may be present with brain-based challenges such as ADHD, anxiety, depression, hoarding disorder, post-traumatic stress disorder, and traumatic brain injury."*

The Institute of Challenging Disorganization, an educational non-profit organization, began as The National Study Group on Chronic Disorganization in 1992. Its mission is to provide education, research, and strategies to benefit people affected by CD and the professionals who work with them. I have witnessed CD in many forms in my professional practice and have found it to be one of the most misunderstood conditions among my clientele. Thier website is www.challengingdisorganization.org

A difficult life transition such as a loss of a loved one may have brought this on. Brain-based conditions such as depression, anxiety, or attention deficit disorder can be a cause of chronic disorganization as well as addictive tendencies. Traditional organizational methodology may not be a good fit for you, but having a non-judgmental support person working with you one-to-one may be just the thing to springboard you into an organized life.

> For more information on hoarding disorder and chronic disorganization, these sites offer resources and guidance:
>
> The Institute for Challenging Disorganization:
> www.challengingdisorganization.org
>
> National Institute for Mental Health:
> https://www.nimh.nih.gov/
>
> The OCD Foundation:
> iocdf.org

Photographic Memories

I Create some stories now in your albums—as busy as you are—so your older self will be grateful and proud of you. This is easier than you think. Several digital and web-based platforms exist that allow you to comment on a photo in your digital library directly, but I would like you to take this a step further. In your 20s, I asked you to please get very selective about the pictures you keep in your cloud and your life. In your 30s, I invite you to become more mindful about TAKING your photographs. Just like overbuying clothes (see the next section), taking too many pictures and not deleting unnecessary images will only create more work later that you genuinely don't have time to do. Hanging out in the weeds of all those unwanted photos for hours trying to find the one you want to keep is time-consuming and emotionally exhausting.

I currently have 84 selfies. I'm semi-ashamed. But the good news is that I had 872. The 84 I have are AWESOME shots of me. Be brave. You can do it!

I've always found that I get more traction on large, overwhelming projects when I have company. I used to go on little scrapbooking weekends with my friends, and we would each spend hours being productive, sorting out our memories, telling and finally writing down the stories of what was happening in those photos. We would have so much fun, and the dedicated time we set aside four times a year made us feel like we could accomplish our photo organizing and album-making goals. If you can't take a whole weekend, try to set aside one day a month when you can take at least three hours to curate your photos.

CHRONOLOGICAL ORDER

Your Financial and Professional Goals

Allow me to be raw here and share with you why I'm passionate about being intentional about this stage of your life. I had gotten married at a young age by today's standards. I was 24. By 25, I had my first child, and four years later, my second child was born. At 32, we upgraded to the dream home with all the bells and whistles. By 34, I was pregnant and separated. The dream house was up for foreclosure! You see, from the time of the closing on that house, something snapped in my husband! The thought of having to pay that debt for the next 30 years was at the forefront of his mind. He obsessed about the expense. So much that it caused him to spiral down, living in a constant state of worry and fear. It gnawed at him, and instead of being happy and loving our dream house, he began to hate it and regret ever buying it. With the bigger house came larger utility bills, and even though we could afford it all, the pressure got in his head. Then came the surprise of having our third child, one we didn't plan on having seven years after our second child was born (yes, I was that 2% who got pregnant while taking the birth control pill—this is a real thing!). The overwhelm consumed my husband to the point of such a deep depression that he eventually stopped working altogether. He checked out, and with that, I was left with no choice but to pick up, pack up, and leave that dream house behind. I had to get a studio apartment for my soon-to-be three children and pray he would wake up and join us among the living again!

You see, the house we thought we must have or needed to have wasn't what we needed at all! It wasn't worth my husband's sanity! We remained separated until he got himself well shortly before our third child was born. Things you never imagined would happen. They often come when we're just going through the motions and not being the watchmen on the

> tower of our kingdoms! When we lost our house, and we were in the pit, we had to take a hard look at how we allowed ourselves to fall into it. What we discovered was that we were the ones who were digging that big hole all along by not being intentional and planning our lives together. We decided that if we were capable of digging that hole together, we could fill it back up together, and we worked hard to rebuild our family.

REALITY CHECK
Life has curveballs.

J Second guessing is normal for all of us before we make a big decision. I need you to try very hard not to beat yourself up or get too wrapped up in the choices you made by calling them mistakes. Acknowledge the decisions you made, and vow to make more informed and thought-over ones in the future. When you made those decisions, you were armed with only what you knew at the time and did the best you could. We've all done it. Did I make the right choice by not going to grad school? Was it wise to go into social work, have a baby at 24, and another at 26? I don't think I thought about long-term consequences then. For instance, the baby is yours *forever*—so that means the rest of that baby's life you'll worry about that person and want them to be okay, emotionally AND financially. I don't think when I was pregnant I considered that the baby would become a toddler, a young child, then go to school, and so on and so forth. I hadn't considered for a moment that I would fall in love with these little people so much and abandon my goal of furthering my education. I LOVED being their mother, and I loved motherING. I enjoyed managing the household, preparing meal plans, and helping them learn their colors, numbers, letters, and shapes. I made healthy snacks, did laundry and ironing with JOY, played "trains" and "grocery store", and danced and sang with those little people every day.

My only regret during that time is that I did very little college planning for THEM because of my low income and lack of knowledge. I didn't think I "qualified" to save very much, and in my thirties, when they were starting to go to school, I created a tiny 529 Plan for each child. When they went off to college, it helped, but it wasn't nearly enough to cover a semester, let alone four years of tuition.

I really didn't think about one moment past the one I was in. This is a good thing when it comes to being present with the people you love but not so great if you aren't planning your next financial steps or goals. Being caught later in life with your financial pants down is absolutely no fun.

Ask yourself these questions:

- Do you need an advanced degree to further your career?
- Do you have time to dedicate to learning?
- Do you have the resources to purchase tuition costs?
- Do you WANT to learn something new?

Most people progress into the next level of education immediately following their undergraduate degree in their 20s. It just seems natural to slip right into the next phase—get that Master's, get the "good job." If you're pursuing academia as a career, you've gone past the Master's and have that Ph.D. Maybe you're teaching, doing research, or, if in the psychology field, treating clients. Most people who have their Ph.D. are deeply absorbed in their work, mission, and field. Perhaps, now that you're in your 30s, no matter what you decided as your path in your 20s, it's alright to change your direction, either slightly or dramatically. Yes, there is the fact that you'll have to tell your family and friends that you're not happy with your career choice. But here's the thing, and it's a big thing: You are not a tree. You can move. You can go somewhere else and do whatever makes you excited and happy.

In your 30s, you may still be carrying debt from college. This is normal! However, if it's something weighing you down and causing stress, try to find a way to restructure your debt. Visit your bank or see your financial advisor. There's usually a lower interest rate or creative solution to consolidate and lower debt of all kinds. Refinancing usually has some fees attached, but the long-term gain is generally worth it.

Here's my sage advice: **Always advance in some way.** Find what excites you and get better at it. Get stronger in your knowledge. Even if you decide to stay home and raise children, you can still move toward your education goals—take an online course, take a credit course at a local college at night or during the day when the kids are at school. Find an online study group that relates to your interests. If you can't afford graduate school, this is more than okay. You don't need to go into bankruptcy to learn! You can learn for free from podcasts, community colleges, online "Master Classes" (usually led by celebrities and notables), and so on. You can also take one class at a time toward a degree if that works better for you. The point is: Advance yourself. When and if you decide you want to pursue more work in your field, your knowledge will be sharp and ready to be applied.

You need to highlight this sage advice from Jill! Never stop learning. Every day I make it a point to learn something new. With a simple search on Google, you can learn how to do just about anything! So many free courses and tutorials. Your mind needs to be stimulated, and there's no age limit on learning. I recently learned how to change the spark plugs and light bulbs in my car. A quick search on YouTube, and I found a step-by-step instructional video that was so easy to follow. I got under that hood, and within an hour, I saved myself $400.00. To be honest, I felt pretty proud of myself. It felt good to get a bit greasy and learn a little more about how my car actually ran. Knowledge is power, and it can save you a lot of money!

If you haven't met with a financial advisor yet, NOW is the time. Beyond this decade, it truly becomes dangerous for your future not to start saving now. Your advisor will be able to determine your risk comfort level and will be able to set up your retirement goals with you at your first meeting. How much do you need versus want to live on are usually VERY different numbers.

If you're not sure of the difference between what you need and want, let me help a little. Here are some basic guidelines as to what a need versus a want is:

Chronological Order

Need money for:

- rent/mortgage
- utilities (no, cable is not a utility; gas, phone, electric, water, and oil are considered utilities)
- food
- clothing (but careful here—no more than what fits in your closets, drawers, and on shelves) for work, play, and exercise
- transportation (to work or to care for others)—this could be a moderately priced used car or public transportation
- medical expenses for yourself and any dependent family members
- toiletries (haircare, personal care, essentials)
- home maintenance (plumbing, roof repair, HVAC repair or replacement, gutter cleaning, etc.)
- savings (even a little bit helps)
- education to further your career goals and increase future wages
- emergency fund (three to six months of your annual income is recommended)

Want money for:

- home improvement supplies: paint, wallpaper, hardware, window coverings, etc.
- home decor
- dining out
- entertainment (shows, video games, movies, winery/brewery tours, museums, and amusement park tickets are some examples)
- cocktails/drinks out with friends
- parties at your house/entertaining
- a brand new car (trust me, these lose their value the MOMENT you drive off the lot)
- more clothing, shoes, and accessories than you need for work, play, or exercise
- gifts
- vacation/travel
- books not related to education

YOUR THIRTIES

J *Design your life, reduce your stress.* How do you like to spend your time now? (If you answered that you have no free time—whoa. You must have SOME. Like, when you use social media of any kind, you're using your free time. When you binge-watch Netflix, you have free time. When you read more than five sentences of a book, you're using your free time. You get the idea.)

We're all given the same 24 hours in a day, and we all get to choose how we spend them.

Usually, when I ask my clients to list the top five ways they would like to spend their time, and then ask them to list the five activities they do most during the day, they rarely line up. Here's a sample:

Desired Activities:
- quality time with my kids/family every day
- writing in my journal every day
- running/walking regularly
- playing with the dog outside every day
- spending time with my friends/calling them weekly to see how they are

Actual Activities:
- working past regular hours (a.k.a. workaholic, not overtime with pay)
- choir member at church
- book club coordinator
- writing/editing a blog for a friend to help her business
- running group team member

You can see by these activities that there are some threads of them that overlap with the values—somewhat. For instance, if you think that the runner is honoring his or her running and walking value regularly, you're right. However, a runner who's in a running group commits to showing up on a regular basis to help the other people in his or her group to show up, too—it's an accountability and herd culture that I fully support. (I'm in a running group.) The rub is when the running sessions become so frequent that it violates the other values, such as time with the family or taking time away from writing in that journal. This lack of following our heart's pursuits leads to stress and frustration, which can spiral into depression and anxiety and a whole lot of other not-so-fun consequences of not using our values to guide our activities.

Let's look at the choir member who loves singing and enjoys the social aspect of being with his or her fellow choir members every week, sometimes two or three times a week, especially during the holidays. The regular weekly commitment is about five hours (two-hour practice, one and a half hours of performance time, and then one hour commuting twice a week to the church, with a bit of wiggle room in there for socializing before and after practice). It's an honorable and rewarding thing to do for the church community! HOWEVER, where does it say "singing for church" in the values list above? It doesn't.

Moreover, if the people in the choir are the only group of friends one has, then it matches the social part of the "values list" very well. This is usually not the case, though, because by the time we're in our thirties, we have friends from high school, college, work, and the neighborhood. We might have even expanded our social circles to include other young parents. I don't want you to quit the choir, by the way, or stop running every week. I'm only asking you to look at how you spend your time and how it conflicts with the values you've determined are important to your identity and contentment.

Regarding the Book Club Secretary position that someone might have been bamboozled into because they're "very organized" and "so good at it!" (this reminds me of my days in the PTA), remember this: Reading is what that person values, not voluntarily being in charge of other readers. If you're sending out reminders and sign-up sheets, you're NOT playing with your dog. If you're writing a blog for a friend because you're helpful AND talented, you're not writing in your own journal. See the pattern?

If you're sitting at a cute little restaurant table frantically looking on your phone to see who's coming to book club in two weeks, you're telling your seven-year-old (non-phone-holding) kid to "hold on a minute, sweetie" while you look at your phone for RSVP emails and she's patiently sitting across from you, and you're definitely NOT engaging with her for BOOK CLUB. By the way, I've seen this at restaurants that the child just sits there being a good, quiet, and patient child. For 15 minutes or more, just sitting, looking up at the ceiling, at other people, maybe drawing or playing on an iPad. I just want to vomit because I probably did this to my kids years ago for work emails and texts. We didn't have iPads back then, so they were probably drawing on a Denny's placemat with a pen from my purse or counting sugar packets while I looked at a tiny screen believing that responding before the next business day made me some kind of superhero. I still have guilt about these less-than-wonderful moments in my life. There was nothing more important than that moment with my kids, and I blew it. For WORK EMAILS. Ouch.

Everyone needs to be *intentional* about taking time to rest. Studies now prove that downtime replenishes the brain's stores of attention and motivation. Rest encourages productivity, creativity, and is essential to achieve our highest levels of performance. Additional studies have proved that our brains' peak performance can only handle about four hours of work. Any activity beyond that's futile, and you've now entered into what I refer to as *"stinkin' thinkin' mode."* It's best to be honest with yourself at this point; unplug and step away from your desk; you're checked out!

>"If you get tired, learn to rest, not to quit" - Banksy

After months and months of planning the very first Launch Collective EXPO in Pittsburgh, I needed to give my brain time to wander and recover. **A wandering mind unsticks us. Intentional times of rest allow us to process, learn from the past, and plan for our future.** I decided that I would take an entire month off from work, something I've never done, and just rest! It ended up being one of the most productive things I've done for myself and my business in a long time!

CHRONOLOGICAL ORDER

My time of rest took me through what I now refer to as "***The 7 R's***". They are:

1. **Recharge**
2. **Reassess**
3. **Realign**
4. **Remove**
5. **Recalibrate**
6. **Refocus**
7. **Resume**

During this time, I allowed my body and mind to *recharge*; it felt awesome to not wake up to an alarm clock and have no set agenda for my day. I spent my time relaxing and stepping outside of the day-to-day routines I usually follow.

As I allowed my mind to unwind and wander, I first observed that I was naturally *reassessing* my life. Thinking about what I had just accomplished, what I was pleased with, what I would like to change, and a stream of new ideas began to flow.

I spent a lot of time in a comfy chair taking notes and jotting down my thoughts and ideas. A fresh perspective, and a new direction emerged. A *realignment* of my goals and plans was laid out on the pages before me.

What came next was an observation of what activities were no longer serving my business and my life that needed to be *removed* or changed. I also noted activities that were still beneficial to me but now needed to be *recalibrated* or dialed in a bit to produce the new outcome for which I now was aiming.

I had a *refocused* plan now in place and was pumped up with the energy to *resume* my work. I challenge you to do the same! Schedule and take some time off and allow yourself permission to do nothing!

Your Relationships and Social Life

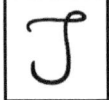 A note to my fellow Type A/Workaholics: If you're trying to make more money, working longer hours not only doesn't achieve that (especially if you're salaried), it takes a considerable chunk out of your relationships with your significant other, your friends, and your

kids if you have them. You also lose a lot of time you would and should use to regroup, recharge, and plan ahead. One of the loudest regrets I hear from people my age and beyond is that they didn't take care of themselves or enjoy more moments with their favorite people in the world for the sake of advancement and financial gain. Setting boundaries around those long work hours will only benefit you and, subsequently, those you love.

I also have to say that "work/life balance" can be a comical goal. I ask my clients to have "not too much of a bad thing" and slowly release the activities from their lives that hurt their values. Adding activities that complement your values (like the running group once a week) and subtracting what conflicts with your values (practicing and performing in a choir six hours per week) will reduce your stress (conflict between your activities and your values) and increase your quality of life. That's what we all want, isn't it (besides world peace and a healthy planet)?

If you have a partner you live with and share the responsibilities for your home and any children you're raising together, you have to work on roles you'll each take on. Most people naturally fall into their responsibilities, and this isn't always best. Stereotypically and historically, men worked outside the home, and women kept the inside of the house running. With gender equality and identification breaking those norms into a bunch of tiny little pieces, it's not odd to see a wife and mother weeding the sloping front yard and cutting the grass while the father and husband is feeding the baby and running to the grocery store to fulfill the menu he planned for the week. I love just about everything about this! However, no matter what you WANT to do and what you each really love doing around the home, sometimes the balance of the chores may fall to one person.

This is primarily due to personality traits, like those who do so much (and possibly later resent it) are enabling and people-pleasing by nature. It's challenging for these people to say NO. They're givers, and maybe they won't regret saying yes, but it eats up a lot of their time to keep doing things FOR everyone else but themselves. These people will see their lives pass them by very quickly and will possibly, at the age of 40 or later, ask themselves where the time went, and before you know it, they can slip into a midlife crisis, with or without resentment.

CHRONOLOGICAL ORDER

So if you're in the 30s and reading this section, divide up the chores, rotate the ones you both hate doing so that bitterness doesn't develop, and make sure you take time for each other and all that you both enjoy doing. Do you remember those? No? Try. Try hard to remember what you liked doing before joining hands and deciding to commit to a lifetime together. Go back and remember the bliss and total rapture you felt when you played basketball with friends on Tuesday night, shopped and had lunch with friends on a Sunday, or read books in the bathtub now and then. These are all choices you can make before that Regret Train leaves the station and you find yourself angry for no reason when you see a basketball, friends having lunch and laughing, or your poor, lonely bathtub (which you only use to shower in for less than five minutes per day since you're running late, again).

In the interest of getting to know ourselves and our partners a little bit better, take a moment and fill out the short exercise on the next page:

"Take Five"

Write down five things you like doing (just YOU):

1.
2.
3.
4.
5.

Write down five things you both enjoy doing TOGETHER:

1.
2.
3.
4.
5.

 I love that Jill has us thinking of how we merge our identities as a couple. This is vital to a lasting relationship. Communicating our needs and desires and delegating household responsibilities every week will keep your family thriving.

Speaking of a thriving relationship, when was the last time you and your spouse had sex? Yes, I went there. I know, I know you're just so exhausted from work and after reading Goodnight Moon for the third time that you fell asleep in your toddler's bed. But don't take the intimacy of your marriage for granted. You and your spouse need time to be intimate. It's crucial that you and your partner model a passionate relationship for your children. There's no greater gift that you can give your children than the security that comes from you both being madly in love with one another. Make date night a priority and budget in alone time. Let your kids see an example of a couple who truly enjoys each other and values time together. It's easy to fall into this pattern of constantly putting your children's needs above the needs of each other. But I'm telling you, your kids need to know that the world doesn't revolve around them. The health of your relationship comes first, and out of that, together, you can raise children in the security of a happy home with committed parents who love each other. A healthy relationship requires you to keep the fire burning. It's a blessing to have a wonderful marriage and a fantastic sex life, not to mention all the wonderful health benefits. So, make love often!

 **About Your Parents**
In your 30s, your parents might seem much like you—immortal. They're only in their 50s or 60s, and if you have kids, they're officially grandparents. It's easy to assume your parents

are eager to watch those little cherubs, and believe me, grandkids are AMAZING. It's important to keep in mind that this is their time to finally do all the things they were dreaming of while raising their own children (yes, you). If you have the resources, invite your nanny or a caregiver on family trips so your parents can enjoy both their family time and some "alone time." If you don't have the resources, just figure out which nights will be "in" and which nights you can rotate some "kid-free" time out and about. There's always a compromise! Having open communication about their needs and coming up with a schedule that makes everyone happy is an excellent idea, don't you think?

I say this next part with the utmost respect for you and for them. If you need a babysitter, and they live nearby, they're going to have a hard time telling you no. They'll want to help you and to save you money. But here's the thing: They already raised their kids (you) and helped form you into who you are today. They did all the stuff you're doing right now that you potentially need a break from. I get it! I did it! Let them have their time now. If they offer, that's one thing. Maybe they're bored, or perhaps they genuinely want to help, but keep in mind that they're trying to figure out their life, too. They might be widowed or divorced and trying to make their way in the world alone. The cure isn't going to be watching your kids four days a week to "give them something to do." There's always a compromise, like watching your kids one day a week when the children are too sick to go to school or daycare or you have a big meeting or a work deadline, etc.

Thank you, Jill, for making this point! I'm considered a young grandmother. I'm only 54, and for many years I helped my daughter, who was a single mom at the time, watch the kids while she went to work. We actually "co-parented." My daughter would go in to work from 3 P.M. to 11 P.M. I can tell you I love my daughter and grandchildren. But at the age of 50, I was physically exhausted. There's a reason most women have their babies in their late 20s and 30s. Also, as much as I loved being with my grandkids, it was challenging because most of my friends were now socializing more because they had become empty-nesters or were soon to be. Now that my daughter lives in her own home and is soon to be married, I like that I can spend a few nights a month with the grandkids or have them over for the weekend for quality time. If you need childcare, then be sure you have it set up before the baby is born.

LIFE ESSENTIALS:
Things to have in place before you're 39:

- Updated Life Insurance - Review insurance and investments. Adjust or modify coverage—you now have more stuff!
- Updated Wills - Review and modify if more children have been born or if you have any marital or property changes.
- Updated Living Will (see Life Essentials Chapter)
- Updated Vital Records (see Life Essentials Chapter)
- Updated Power of Attorney
- Updated Home Inventory
- Updated Health Benefits
- Updated Care and Living Plan

YOUR FORTIES

Your Identity and Well-being

When we reach our 40s, we now feel like we've mastered this thing called life. We're much more relaxed in our roles as parents, wives, and husbands. This is the season of what I call the COMFORT ZONE. You've lived life; now you're the one who's sharing your recipes, tips, and experiences with the newlyweds at church. You have confidence in running a household. Every morning you can do two loads of laundry and throw a meal in the Crockpot before you even walk out the door for work each day. Each year you throw one heck of a Christmas party for the neighbors and host an even greater 4th of July barbecue. Your friends and neighbors on social media think you're living the dream! At work, you could do your job in your sleep; you've transitioned into being an expert in your field. And through the day-to-day of all of this, you even managed to survive teaching your 16-year-old how to drive! Life is feeling quite comfortable—or is it?

On the outside, this all looks pretty awesome, but be careful here. It's also in our 40s that discontentment begins to creep in, and life can become mundane. The routines can start to feel monotonous. Relationships become stagnant. It's so easy to slip into roles and patterns that we somehow get too comfortable in. We then do the math and wonder how we reached being middle-aged! Be aware: The "midlife crisis" happens. You wonder how you and your spouse haven't had a meaningful conversation other than "What do you want for dinner?" and "Do you need anything from the store?" Somewhere in all this living, you lost the passion for your life. The COMFORT ZONE isn't all it's cracked up to be. If you want your marriage and family to continue to be healthy, you need to be mindful of this. It's during this time that many married couples head to divorce court.

Very quickly, life as you know it can change. The change often comes in our late 40s, when we start to notice that our parents are slowing down or have been diagnosed with a health issue. In the blink of an eye, we somehow become "sandwiched" between work, running our own households, and helping to care for our elders. It's time to have some honest conversations about aging and how you can navigate through this time of your lives.

YOUR FORTIES

You no longer have time to put things off!

If you picked up this book, you're a small percentage of people who take the time to educate themselves early before a crisis. We've given it our best shot to start preparing you. It's been our hope that you've taken our advice and have done what we suggested you do through the earlier decades of your life. If you have not reviewed the Life Essentials in the back of this book, now is the time! The crisis usually shows up in your 50s, and trust me you're going to be very glad you listened to me and took care of that list!! So make those essential appointments with your financial planner, meet with an estate attorney, and host a family meeting with your parents and siblings to dig in and have some of the vital conversations before someone falls and breaks a hip or has a heart attack. I can't emphasize it enough.

J | This stage of your life has many milestones (besides celebrating your 40th birthday and planning your midlife crisis). You may be experiencing a career peak, and if you have teenage and adult children, they may be reaching major milestones of their own—graduations, relationships, beginning college. Your car used to cart around soccer balls, dirty kids, and groceries. With older kids, you probably feel that not much has changed, but the mall and Friday night football games are the more popular destinations than the soccer fields or the local park. There might be conversations in that car that no longer rotate around their grades and their mean math teacher. The casual conversations might become disguised as a lot of little lectures about the importance of birth control, a nice group of friends as a circle of influence, and, of course, staying off drugs. Recreational drugs might be considered safe or unsafe to you as a parent, especially if your kids know you partake from time to time or used to enjoy the herb when you were young. If you use recreational drugs yourself and they know this, you might want to leave that last part out. Either way, having an open and judgment-free discussion about drugs, their effects (physically, emotionally, and socially) is a sensible thing to do.

If you stayed home to raise children or even worked part-time from home, now is the time where you may be rejoining the workforce full time, which brings a whole new set of house rules and time-management challenges (even if you still get to work from home). You may be processing papers and bills on the weekends, where before, you did this frequently throughout the week with a more flexible schedule. Planning meals can be more challenging than ever, with so many people in the house going in so many different directions.

Meal Planning Basics
In your 20s, I shared with you what to keep as pantry basics. Having those items on hand will save you from smacking yourself across the face when you get home from the grocery store, realizing you forgot those things and you need them for a recipe, like right now.

In terms of planning meals themselves, there can be an element of fun in this. I like to mix it up (pardon the pun). I try to make the standard fare of meals I won't mess up, and if there's something new I want to try, like a vegan meal (and I'm not even vegan! How hipster am I?) or a new side dish, I take the time to experiment on only one of these per week. Go online or grab a cookbook from the library and pick out at least four new recipes you want to try. If you go online, most sites allow you to create a grocery list from the recipe itself. I love this feature. If anyone else can do the thinking for me, I'm all for it! I'm not very adventurous in the kitchen, but some people are. If you're anything like me, I strongly encourage you to make lower-ingredient meals with easy and straightforward prep steps.

When the kids were still sleeping on Sunday mornings, I had a routine of planning four meals per week and creating the grocery lists. I always organize (to this day) my shopping list into the departments I can find the items in (i.e., produce, seafood, dairy) so I don't look and feel like a human pinball once I'm in the store. I had it timed pretty well and was in and out with my airtight plan within one hour.

Cook on the weekend and freeze as many meals as you can in advance. Weeknights, when you're too busy and tired to cook, you can just quickly put together what you prepared.

When it's time for the bird(s) to finally fly off to college or to move in with friends, the wave is climbing higher now, the momentum is here, and it's all for you! Preparing for an "empty nest" is one of those activities that some people enjoy doing (like planning on what exactly to do with that bedroom—a workout room? a reading room? a HUGE closet?), OR they completely dread it and begin considering ways in which to make that room a veritable time capsule.

Empty nesting is one of the strangest phenomena in the world. I liken it a little to going off to college, for me. One minute I'm terrified and on the verge of tears about the unknown. The next moment I'm running around with so much unmitigated freedom on my hands, I scarcely know what to do with myself. (I wrote this last bit after watching a LOT of British television, so bear with me.) One of the silver linings of empty nesting is that the time you usually spent parenting directly (you'll always be parenting indirectly, from afar, trust me) can now be spent on YOUR interests and goals and YOUR space!

Here's a pivotal point in your midlife years. Either you:

- Have a midlife crisis where you purchase things you don't need and enhance your outward appearance to seem younger, even to yourself **OR**
- Have a midlife **upgrade** to redesign your next decades, including getting healthier in your mind, body, and environment.

I personally chose the latter and learned how to surf when I was 45, becoming much better at it by the time I was 50. Living really, really, really far inland, this took a lot of planning to get to coasts, but I did it and continue it still. Many of my friends were shocked when I took up surfing. People joked with me, telling me my midlife crisis was sure unique! (That was hysterical and amusing.) Anyway, I'm still surfing and getting better at it all the time. I will surf until I die (dude).

Mind: Mental health is JUST as important as physical health and wellness. In your 40s, there are new issues that come to play and many life changes yet again. Somehow these are different. Besides dealing with watching our parents age and change, we're also coping with stress in an entirely new way, if we're coping at all. Some people use food and alcohol to get by, and some people head to the gym. Some do both. Finding a healthy way to cope with life's problems

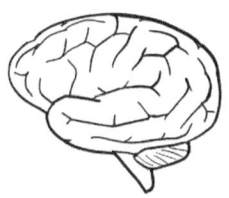

is an age-old challenge. My best advice at this age is to talk to people about your stuff. Openly and authentically share your worries, get ideas, and listen to people you trust—people who like and love you. These people care about your well-being and want you to be happy and feel good. They want you to be at peace, and they're always in your corner. Find at least ONE of these people to run to when you feel blue or need a shoulder to lean on (or cry on, in my case). You don't have to be the same person for them, as they ideally can reach out to others for help and a gentle, understanding ear. By the way, you can still have your own "issues" and be of help to others when they're having a tough time, just by being present—listening, caring, being there.

For those of you who have relationships that aren't making your life better or happier, consider that relationship closely. I've taught groups of people in my life about how toxic people, or even people who don't make us feel good, can be considered clutter. Peter Walsh, a professional organizer and author of *Lose the Clutter, Lose the Weight,* defines clutter as "anything that gets between you and the life you want to be living." He adds to this definition something that most people overlook when they decide to get organized. Walsh states that clutter "could be the physical stuff…or it can be a past emotion, like anger, or any of those mental or emotional things that cripple you or put a hurdle between you and your goals."

If you need more support, it's out there in the forms of therapists and counseling centers, and more acutely, in the ways of telephone hotlines and your health insurance helpline. *Please reach out and get help when you need it. The act of telling someone your story to begin to heal from any trauma, or any brain-based diagnosis, or for anything that's on your mind, is incredibly worth the effort. I've had several different instances in my life where I received help, usually after the death of a family member or after I went through many changes in a short amount of time. I didn't have the ability to cope with the tremendous grief and stress I was experiencing, and with the help of a therapist and some medication, I was able to learn how to deal with and heal from life's many curves and sharp turns.*

Body: Weight is hard as "H.E. double hockey sticks" to get off in this decade (we've pledged not to swear in this book). If you started a great exercise regimen in your 30s, you should be okay. Keep going. If you didn't, it's cool. Do it now. It will feel like you're walking uphill in quicksand for the first few weeks (or even months) of getting in shape, but it's worth it! I thought being a runner would get and keep me in shape for my older years. It sort of did. But I left out a bunch of stuff, like eating healthy foods and using weights to build fat-burning muscle. I also, with all my newfound free time, really enjoyed having cocktails and wine, along with delicious food I thought I could eat because I ran so much. Well, let me reach into my big bag of "nope"s and say "nope" to that.

When my doctor told me gently "not to gain any more weight" as I neared 50, I hired a fitness coach. The nice thing about being in your late 40s is that you have some cash to pursue your fitness goals, like hiring a fitness coach. A fitness coach can help you restyle your nutrition and exercise routines, not just encourage you to do "ten more" burpees or other forms of torture in the gym. I completely upended all I was doing (including spending too much time watching the Hallmark channel with chips and guac) and started putting only good stuff in and treating myself when I wanted to the things I really enjoyed. The effort was and is the best thing I do with my time. I work out in some fashion once a day—either running or doing some High-Intensity Interval Training (HIIT) with weights or not. It has changed everything. When my coach said my "program was a marathon, not a sprint," he was 100% accurate. This was a complete lifestyle shift over a period of time that I allowed myself to have, including forgiveness for that dessert on vacation or that extra fancy cocktail when out with friends. I absolutely love who I am when I'm taking good care of myself, and when I'm not, guess what? I still love myself. I just forgive the behavior and move on. Do I keep three sizes of pants in my closet? You betcha. The ones I wear, the ones I don't want to wear, and the ones I will wear again. It's okay! I love being human.

Your Home and Your Space

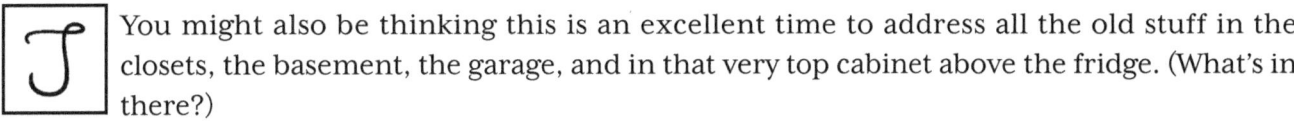 You might also be thinking this is an excellent time to address all the old stuff in the closets, the basement, the garage, and in that very top cabinet above the fridge. (What's in there?)

There's also the matter of your parents giving you furniture and stuff they don't want anymore that they think YOU need. Sigh. You take it, begrudgingly but smiling, and put it in your car, then the garage. Five years later—or, okay, 20—it's still there, out of guilt or total abject fear that your mom will see you aren't using that lamp she gave you for your office last year. Maybe you can put a blanket over it the next time she comes…or you could donate it instead and brace yourself. (She'll still love you if you give away the lamp.)

I used a technique in my busiest moments in this hugely challenging decade of my life that helped me focus with great success, and it bears repeating in this chapter: O.H.I.O.—Only Handle It Once.

When reviewing each item during your sorting and decluttering process, hold it in your hand and process what it is, what its purpose is, and what feelings, if any, it evokes. Touching the item, even furniture, will help you feel as if you've fully processed the item's place in your home and, frankly, your heart. Putting the item in your hands also makes it easier to put it in the next "right place," which is either a donate box, a recycle bin (if it's paper or electronics), or a sell bag. If it's a "keeper,"  take it directly to the place where you believe you'll use it the most. This is a process we call "zoning." If it gets close to where it will be enjoyed and utilized, it's more likely to be pulled into the everyday mix of your life. Only then will you know if it was a good idea to keep it or not. But here's the true magic of this step: You can only touch it once before deciding its fate. Do NOT pick it up until you're genuinely ready to make a decision.

If you haven't unpacked from your last move, no judgment here! But it's important to find out what's in those boxes and deal with the contents. Hiring a professional organizer is an excellent idea in general, but when there's a backlog of stuff like those old boxes, it's imperative to have a professional at your side to drive accountability and increase the likelihood that you'll really and properly make those much-delayed decisions about what to keep and what to release.

If you've lovingly curated more than you meant to keep from your children's lives, here's a tip on how to consolidate those artifacts:

Create ONE bin for each of the three stages of life that they lived in your home:

Bin #1: Baby to Kindergarten Years, or 0-5
Bin #2: School Years, or 6-13
Bin #3: High School Years, or 14-18

That's it! If it doesn't fit in the bins, it doesn't get to stay. If you have flat and large artwork, grab a portfolio keeper from a craft or art store, label it with your child's name, and put all those works of genius and talent behind a dresser, in a closet, or under a bed until they can come to claim it all. It's enjoyable and fun to look at your kids' stuff WITH them. We've had so many laughs and tears through the years when we go through their school letters and little projects, along with their unidentifiable clay or dough sculptures.

Another technique I use with our Professional Organizing clients is to take a photo of the unique items, individually or collectively, and make a special photo book out of it. This works with kids as well as with people downsizing a household full of trinkets and memories. Think of it like one of those books you might buy at an art museum. Your child's photo can go on the same pages as the art so he or she can see how old they were when they made their masterpieces. The activity of making this book is priceless, as it gives you both some time together, as well as teaching the child how to make decisions as they age about what matters most to them.

Your Financial and Professional Goals

 Let's talk about debt, shall we? You probably have this under control, but if you don't, this is the decade where you get a fresh start.

If you don't like your job or don't enjoy being an entrepreneur anymore, this is an excellent time to make some significant changes in your career path. If your retirement plan isn't in place, let's get that done. What's a retirement plan? It's a lot more than just a 401(k) (which you should have by now).

Chronological Order

It's an actual plan! Like with a list and everything. If you can plan a meal, you can plan your retirement. I definitely want you to plan out how much money you want or need to have after you stop working altogether, but I think you first need to define how you want to spend that magical time in your life.

What do you like doing in your free time now? Here's my list:

- seeing my kids
- traveling
- reading
- writing
- traveling
- playing my violin
- traveling

Do you see a pattern? What do you think I'll want to do when I retire?

You guessed it, see my family, read, write, play music, and... travel! Yep. So, I better work hard to sock enough money away so I get to spend the rest of my nonworking days doing the things I love with the people I love. You can, too, if you follow our advice. (And, please don't use actual socks. Use a financial advisor or call a banking person you trust.)

If you have kids, do some college planning. If you have a house, grab a notebook or a computer and put all the improvements you want to make on the house in writing. Put in best estimates of how much you think each one will cost using Google as your guide or asking neighbors and friends what they paid, roughly, for their home improvements. Finally, add when you optimally want to install, build, decorate, etc. Having a timeline helps define what "someday" means to you. If you have a partner, make sure you're both on the same page about what you want to save money for. If you're all about replacing the central air conditioning, and your partner is all about Disney World, you may have to make your lists separately and then find common ground. Creating dreams and goals together is fun. The work to get there may not be as much fun, but the reward is incredible. Knowing what you'll need to make your house not only more enjoyable but have top resale value when you're ready to sell will truly help you learn what to set aside each year.

YOUR FORTIES

Is the job you have now the job you'll have forever? Maybe, but as companies evolve and grow, split apart, and rebuild, you may move around quite a bit before you retire. What's important is to make sure you're still earning enough to live on with each change you make but also earning enough to save for the future. The "future" sounds a little nebulous right now and very uncertain, so it's truly hard to know exactly how much you need. Managing what you earn and what becomes of those earnings down the road is a big job.

Reboot Your Budget and Spending

Routine Monthly Money Schedule

- credit card bill review
- debt review
- budget review
- planning for gifts or trips

A little more detail? Okay. Here's a bit more of an explanation of what EVERYONE should be doing once a month to stay healthy, wealthy, and wise.

Check balances of your credit cards: Make a plan to reduce your debt. Your credit utilization amount should be less than 30%. Credit utilization is the term that describes how much of your available credit you're using at any given time. If your credit limit on a card is $4,000 and you currently owe $2,000, you're using 50% of your credit, and that could mean trouble when you apply for a mortgage or seek a car loan looking for a reasonable interest rate. Close down those cards that you're not using, too. Lenders look at how much debt you COULD be in versus how much you're actually in when deciding to let you borrow from their financial institution.

Check your monthly budget: Are you on track? What small changes can you make to keep your promises to yourself? What big things do you want to save up for? A trip? A car? You can do it. I would tell you to trade those expensive cocktails in for saving $50 here and there, but I can't tell you to do something I never would. I can sacrifice clothing purchases for up to six months. I go on spending diets all the time. It doesn't mean I don't occasionally get the cute boots at Macy's, especially if they're marked down 70%, or grab a pair of jeans the next size up (or down, depending on my weight at the time). It just means I'm mindful of what I'm doing with my money. There are apps GALORE on fixing your spending budget.

As long as you enter what you spend, you can watch how close you're getting to your limits. I enter my food into my diet app, and it tells me the calories, nutrients, and properties of the food I am about to eat, so I don't overdo the carbs, the calories, etc. I have to type in the food item or scan the barcode of the package what I'm eating for this to be effective. I'm diligent with this, as I'm currently aware of how middle age and menopause can wreak havoc on my weight. Have I gone over my calorie budget? Yes. Am I more aware of that budget now that I touch it every day? Yes. So, **look at your money every day.** EVERY DAY. Become intimate with it.

Look at the calendar ahead: There should be NO surprises in regards to gift giving. People have had the same birthdays for their whole lives. The holidays are going to happen every year around the same time. Weddings—well, you have at least six weeks to save up for those, and babies, nine months. You get the idea. Use that calendar and start making some decisions about an annual gift budget when you put together your spending allowance. Start setting the funds aside or make sacrifices now so you can afford what you want to spend on that person or place.

Vacations: Where do you want to go? What do you want to see? What kind of memories do you want to bring home? Be specific because it will help you put together an amazing trip for yourself and your travel companions. One of the best sites I found when trying to see how much a trip will cost is Budget Your Trip. Travelers worldwide contribute to this so website visitors have an idea of what they can expect to spend from Thailand to Tahiti, Anchorage to Australia.

Birthdays: Okay. This one is interesting. We usually buy gifts because we love someone and want them to have something unique and that they'll enjoy having, something they look at, or use, or wear and know YOU were the hero—YOU bought that for them! YOU are amazing! YOU are thoughtful! The reality is, gift giving is tricky. Determining a budget for that person is more challenging. How do you put a price on love? How do you show someone you love them with a meager gift budget? I also know you probably have more than one person you love. If you multiply that love by the number of gifts you have to buy, and then…well, you're officially out of money. The credit cards get cracked open to cover these gifts. You promise to pay off those Christmas gifts by March. Then you crack a tooth. March becomes June. Then your significant other gets an invitation to a graduation party. The checkbook comes out, and that credit card is collecting interest, and the bill is NOT getting paid off. Does your high schooler want to go to Disney with the band? (Why didn't anyone tell me about this earlier? They did. You just missed that little line in the information you received in August in your big packet of band builder fundraising that you were going to look at…later.).

Holidays: For large and blended families, try a gift exchange—Secret Santa is helpful. Have people draw a name out of a bowl. Set a budget. These expectations have to be managed WELL in advance, though, and no cheating or side gifts! Also, try to keep it fun by having it stay a surprise. Life doesn't have many happy surprises, so if you draw a name, don't tell anyone who you have!

Weddings (not your own): The gift you give depends primarily on your relationship with the couple. The average gift price these days is $100. If you bring a guest to the wedding, it might be a good idea to give more in terms of the gift's value since they now have two mouths to feed. If it's a close friend or family member, then I suggest giving even more. There's a formula you can follow of how much more to give on top of the average cost if you're invited to the engagement party (20%), the shower (20%), and the wedding (60%).

Anniversaries (your own): While this is entirely subjective for every couple, I've talked to friends and clients alike, and we all agree—sharing the day together is the one thing they cherish the most. Throw a meal in there, along with a meaningful greeting card or note, and it's a home run. If you really want to give a gift, get something that shows how much you know about your partner—a framed poem by their favorite writer, a gift certificate to a salon they love but never have time/money to go to, or a photo gift of the two of you together.

 Now that Jill has you organized on keeping your finances in order, I need to drop a giant truth bomb here!

70% of people over the age of 65 will need long-term care and supportive services in their lifetime.

The facts do not lie. Thanks to the advances in science, medicine, and technology, we're living longer. In America, there are more people over the age of 60 than under the age of 15. It's estimated that by the year 2040, the percentage of people 65 and older will almost double by 22% of the population from 13% in 2010. In a report published by the U.S. Administration on Aging, "A profile of older Americans, 2014," those needing the most care and support aged 85 and older are slated to triple by 2040.

Additionally, it's reported by the United States Census Bureau that currently 19% of the population, one in five individuals, are living with a disability. Many of these individuals require support from a family caregiver. By 2030, 72.8 million U.S. residents (more than one in five) will be 65 or older.

Numbers do not lie. We're living longer! When you plan for your retirement, you MUST factor in that you or your spouse will more than likely need some help and care in your later years. In my 10 years as a senior advisor, I can tell you that it's only a tiny percentage of families who've taken the time to be educated on the cost of long-term care. The sticker shock alone can cause you to break out in a cold sweat. You're still young enough to do something about this!

When we think of our retirement, we tend to be most concerned about having the money we'll need to enjoy our days traveling or purchasing the cabin in the woods. We calculate how much that bucket list may cost us, but we often don't consider the considerable end-of-life expense ahead of our aging parents (or us).

Below are some national average costs for long-term care in the United States (in 2016, from the Administration on Aging):

$225 a day or $6,844 per month for a semiprivate room in a nursing home
$253 a day or $7,698 per month for a private room in a nursing home
$119 a day or $3,628 per month for care in an assisted-living facility (for a one-bedroom unit)
$20.50 an hour for a health aide
$20 an hour for homemaker services
$68 a day for services in an adult day healthcare center

The cost of long-term care depends on the type and duration of care you need, the provider you use, and where you live (it can be a lot higher in some states). Costs can be affected by certain factors, such as:

- Time of day: Home health and home care services, provided in two-to-four-hour blocks of time referred to as "visits," are generally more expensive in the evening, on weekends, and on holidays.
- Extra charges for services may apply for anything beyond the basic room, food, and housekeeping charges at facilities, although some may have "all-inclusive" fees.
- Variable rates in some community programs, such as adult day service, are provided at a per-day rate but can be more based on extra events and activities.

Have I shocked you here? Do you see why it's vital that you take this into account? This (yes, now) would be a good time to log on to the Social Security Administrations website and request a statement to get your projected Social Security benefit amount. Social Security benefits are much more modest than many people realize; the average Social Security retirement benefit in 2019 was about $1,470 a month, or about $17,640 a year. Now let's go back to those numbers above on what it costs for long-term care services. You had better put this future expense into the saving plan! Do you know if your parents have anticipated and planned for this expense? Have you had a family meeting yet? Have you met with that estate planner yet? What are you waiting for?

And yes, I can hear you now saying, "Well, Laurean, doesn't my health insurance or my mom's Medicare cover this?" NO, IT DOES NOT! and we'll talk more about this later, I promise!

Your Relationships and Social Life

We've been busy! Growing into a mature adult takes a lot of energy and self-reflection (my fancy word for falling on your behind and figuring out a way to stand up again without looking like a complete idiot). Our friendships are different, and we might want to reconnect with friends we lost touch with from "before you had kids" or before your job. I'm betting that if it was a good relationship, or even a great one, finding each other again would be welcomed by them, too. So, go on Facebook, Instagram, and LinkedIn if you lost their number or email. Find your squad and make plans. You'll need these pals in the next couple of decades, if not longer, to see you through and to do fun things with.

Naturally, as we age, we grow! We learn new things about others and ourselves—what we like, we don't like. We care less about what others think about us, and sometimes that includes our partners. This is the age where couples either continue to grow together or they grow apart. The disconnect is real. It happens to everyone! If you truly want to stay joined by matrimony, or if you're not married, by your unwavering commitment to each other, the odds are stacked against you. Many people are getting divorced in this decade. They're possibly straying from the relationship, not just with other people but with other interests.

You can still have separate interests but be deeply committed and connected!

It's entirely possible, and I've seen it happen. I ALWAYS ask my clients, the couple who's been married for over 50 years, exactly HOW they did it. How do they still do it? Have they ever wanted to leave?

Did they ever want to go and start over somewhere else…with someone else? Did they know at the beginning that it would last this long? I needed answers, and the standard response for all these people whom I harassed over the years is:

"We grew together, and we didn't let the small stuff get to us."

What does that mean? Most of the couples described it as they developed common interests along the way and passionately pursued them TOGETHER while still developing their own interests and friendships at the same time. So, if they loved to travel, they did that together. But they also went on friend trips with their best pals. They loved plays and the theater in general, but if the one didn't like the symphony, they went to the symphony with someone who loved it, too.

What's the small stuff? Maybe it's the way she NEVER makes the bed. Maybe the toothbrush is left lying on the sink when there's a perfectly good toothbrush holder sitting RIGHT there (can he not SEE it?). Maybe, just maybe, she rarely makes the clothes actually LAND in the hamper, or it's how his used dental floss doesn't quite make it all the way into the little bathroom trashcan, and you have to TOUCH it to get it there. I mean, I could go on and on. We all could. Anyone who has cohabited with another human being knows all about these violations of human co-existence and can tell me one hundred more. Yet, I've never heard someone say these are deal breakers. What's your deal breaker? Do you have more than one? Does your partner KNOW what it is?

Write it here.

A deal breaking behavior for sure is:

Has your partner broken the deal?

Yes ___ No ___

If you checked yes, whoa, boy, you guys need to talk, talk, talk!

Chronological Order

If you checked no, then figure out what you can do to start appreciating the wonderful things about that person and sharing them. Maybe they don't know how awesome you think they are at cooking or getting stains out of your favorite shirt. Or when they take the dogs out at 6:00 A.M. so you can sleep JUST a bit longer…or when they take the kids for ice cream when you need to have that heart-to-heart phone call with a friend or family member who lives far away. When the big stuff is noted and the small stuff is ignored, it's easier to weather many storms together, such as job losses, mental health problems, health crises, kids leaving the nest, and kids moving away from the town where you live.

If you're single by choice or because of divorce (or because of the death of your partner/spouse), take some time to get to know YOU and what you like to do. Take yourself on dates. Go kayaking and get some ice cream afterward. Maybe you like to hang out at the bookstore for hours on end, drinking coffee and daydreaming. I remember when I went out to dinner by myself for the first time after my divorce and didn't feel compelled to bring a book or look at my phone to feel more important. I just sat there and ate, and nothing terrible or weird happened. Also, single seats are way easier to find at movie theaters, restaurants, and, well, anywhere. After I figured this out, I was well on my way to feeling more confident in my developing role as the Mayor of Divorcee City.

In your late 40s, relationships with other family members begin to change as well. You're now about to release into the world the children you've been raising. This can be a time of tension. Don't worry; it's normal for you to look at your teenage child and wonder if he or she has been replaced by an alien. Your once sweet, obedient child is now outspoken and testing the boundaries. This is a constant battle of your almost-adult children trying to cut the apron strings while you're trying hard to keep them tied tight for fear they may go out and get drunk or come home pregnant. Hold on, this is all normal, and you might be filled with many conflicting emotions because a part of you can't wait for them to leave the nest while the other part of you wonders how it all went by so fast. Remember, your teens are dealing with the conflict, too. They crave their independence from you, all at the same time wishing you would forever make their bed and pack their lunch. Not to mention the constant pressure of "What are you doing after high school?" looming over them. It's a lot for them to deal with on top of their raging hormones! Try to have some grace here for them!

LIFE ESSENTIALS:
Things to have in place before you're 49:

- Updated Life Insurance
- Updated Wills
- Updated Living Will
- Updated Vital Records
- Updated Power of Attorney (see Life Essentials Chapter)
- Updated Home Inventory
- Updated Health Benefits
- Updated Care and Living Plan

YOUR FIFTIES

CHRONOLOGICAL ORDER

Your Identity and Well-being

L   I recently turned 54, and I must say I love being 54. I'm enjoying seeing my children grow into adults, and I even have three grandchildren now. I am blessed. With my home soon to be an empty nest, I've started to think about this next phase of my life. Just a few years ago, I had a household of six, and now it's just my youngest son and me. This past year we downsized from our sizeable four-bedroom home into a two-bedroom apartment. Life has shifted. It's an adjustment, and there are days when I miss the chaos of a full house. It's time for me to embrace the change and create new traditions by allowing my adult children to host the holidays (and enjoy watching them host). I'm embracing the change and enjoying the time I now have to create this next chapter of my life. Soon my youngest will be off to college or out exploring the world on his own. I'm learning how to operate in this new normal. Learning to cook for two instead of six has been a challenge for this Italian woman, but I am learning, and it seems I've come back to the advice I gave you 20-somethings earlier in this book. For myself, I'm DREAMING IT UP BIG once again!

J   Okay, so now you can possibly "see" your age a little more clearly, showing up in all sorts of ways. You might need better, stronger glasses to actually see the changes, but you get the point. You might remember a time you told your friends you wouldn't even consider plastic surgery. You may have even proudly announced, "I'm going to grow old gracefully! I don't want to pretend to be something I'm not!" A lot of people say this in their 30s. Well, now, in this decade of life, that may be a reconsideration. Maybe a little lift here, a little tuck there. I frequently pull up the sides of my face in a mirror and wonder if I should. I probably won't; for the same reason I won't have a tummy tuck. It feels foolish (for me) to get elective surgery when I'm the only living parent my kids have. I can see the funeral now, and all the hushed murmurings and head-shakings: "She looked fine the way she was…didn't need all that work…the grandkids will never know her now because she HAD to look (thinner)(younger)(more attractive) better!" Sigh. Now, this might change. I may reconsider this decision and NOT grow old gracefully. I love/hate seeing photos of myself when I was younger. I love seeing them because I like what I'm doing in the picture and who I'm with. I hate seeing them because I didn't have age spots on my face (they used to be freckles) and so many wrinkles. I took care of my skin, too! I've always used sunscreen, primarily because I'm a redhead, but also to prevent sun damage, which turns into wrinkles, lines, weird marks, and skin cancer. My parents and sister have all had melanoma, so it's common for me to apply zinc oxide when I surf or have sunscreen in my daily makeup.

I'm not sharing this because I'm vain. I'm in the acceptance PHASE of aging. I'm not fully embracing it like Laurean just yet. I'm noticing some limitations. I used to run four to six miles straight, no stopping, with big hills all over the place, at a 9:30 (min/mile) pace. Now I seek flatter courses, feel comfortable if I run three miles, and am exhausted at four. I do a walk/run program where I run for two and a half minutes and walk for 30 seconds until I'm finished, but at an 11 min/mile pace. I'm proud of that. I notice the difference in what I could do in my 30s and 40s. I also notice how much more arduous weight training is, but want to be stronger. So I keep trying, and I keep pushing myself since I'm bound and determined not to get osteoporosis in my later years. Mind you, none of my older female relatives have ANY ailments, including osteoporosis, but it could happen! I take Vitamin D every day because I live in Pittsburgh (the sun shines very seldom here), and I'm supposed to be taking B12, but I keep forgetting. (I'm a professional organizer, so I promise I'll figure this out and add it to my daily routine…somewhere.)

You may notice something happening in your 50s that you didn't experience in your 40s. Here are some fun new things that might occur:

- You schedule doctor's visits for weird stuff that you're experiencing for the first time
- Your friends tell you about their weird doctor stuff—usually during dinner in a nice restaurant—instead of the last episode of "Game of Thrones" (both are important, but one might be more important than the other)
- You have periodic cancer scares (words like "abnormal" and "cells" become more alarming and noticeable when used in the same sentence) every time you have a screening or routine exam
- You turn the radio down more, especially when you're parallel parking, so you can "see better"
- You might reevaluate the lifelong goal to run a full marathon (a 5K sounds pretty good)
- You join book clubs to actually talk about the book

- Spots and other weird stuff show up on your skin (this causes you to pause and watch the face lotion commercials and info ads on Instagram, rather than scrolling past them)
- You start looking at and analyzing same-age celebrities to see how you stack up
- You start going a little more slowly down the stairs in case you "turn your ankle" or, worse, fall.
- You start going up the stairs a little more slowly because, well, arthritis, and you don't want to run
- You wonder if you should start learning Bridge so you can play sort of well in your 70s

> This decade of our lives is a significant turning point...and yes, Jill, I am working on embracing it. Really, I'm learning to love myself. Something I've never been good at throughout my life. I did an okay job of loving others until this point, but in hindsight, I could have loved them oh so much more if I had loved myself first.

Remember earlier, when I said the crisis could hit you in the 50s...well, it did hit me hard shortly after my 50th birthday, when my husband passed away. Earlier, Jill was talking about how couples in their older years talked about how they had successful relationships. My marriage wasn't thriving before my husband died. In fact, we'd been separated for a while before he was diagnosed with cancer. The reality was we weren't going to reconcile and live out our golden years together. I was in the process of meeting with a divorce attorney when we got the news that Bill had Stage 4 cancer of the esophagus. Suddenly I no longer cared so much about all those issues that led us to separation. Our marriage's brokenness seemed to diminish as I chose to focus on just being there for him and my children. The focus became, "Laurean, how are you going to live together as a family the last days of this man's life? How will you support him and help make his last days on earth a little bit better? What memories will you create together with your children, and how will you both be an example to them of forgiveness and compassion?" Are you going to have a successful marriage, 'til death do you part? I can say wholeheartedly I did have a successful marriage in the end.

After my husband died, my children thanked me for all I did for their dad. They knew I had to let go of a lot and forgive him, but more importantly, I had to forgive myself for my role in the breakdown of our marriage. When you lose your spouse, you'll miss them—and oddly enough, the things I miss most about my husband are all those little things that drove me crazy, like his obsession with how you fold a t-shirt.... Oh, how I miss him doing the laundry! Jill is correct; let go of the little things, just love one another, laugh often, and don't go to bed angry!

Today I'm a big advocate for my friends' and family's marriages. You see, imagine if Bill and I had loved each other every day of our lives together like it was our last....

Tomorrow is promised to no one!

J It's hard to imagine, if you're parents, what your next chapter will look like if your home isn't as full as it was. The food shopping changes. The amount of laundry sure does change, and the house is a lot easier to clean. But you'll miss the voices and the TV you asked them to lower the volume on 50 million times. The socks won't be on the steps anymore or buried in the sofa cushions. The remote will always be where you left it, and so will your car keys. It will be so darn odd to have order and all that...quiet.

Chronological Order

J Taking my son to college, my firstborn, all alone, was one of the saddest days of my life. Until…I took my daughter. Then I was really, truly alone. I cried on the way home from each of their colleges. For my son, who only had a suitcase, his guitar, two plastic bins, and a hamper, I just drove straight home, bawling my eyes out. For my daughter, after I unpacked her stuff with her, made her new bed, decorated her room a little, did a grocery and a Target run, returned the U-Haul, and fiercely hugged her goodbye, I was halfway home and through one box of tissues, when I realized I needed gas. I stopped at a gas station and noticed an envelope tucked into my purse. The little bugger must have put it there when I said goodbye without my seeing her. The outside said, in her loopy little handwriting, "When You Are Ready."

OH MY GOD.

I started to cry at the gas pump, right there in front of the convenience store, as I gently opened the envelope and read (through many sobbing, heaving tears) that letter. Mary told me on seven pages of loose-leaf paper what a good job I did raising her. My young, moody, brilliant, and extremely determined girl, who barely talked to me while she was in high school, and only seemed to need me to go shopping with her so I could buy her what she wanted (you know, "mother-daughter time"!) and things like her prom dress, her manicures, and her haircuts. She was responsible, working her job at the senior living community just walking distance away, and helped out around the house after a few eye-rolls, stair-stomping, and door slams. We had moments of fun, though, like our impromptu family dance parties and our coveted movie nights. I loved every moment that she was around, so I was dumbfounded to find out while on a special mother-daughter vacation (in Ireland no less) that I was too "strict". I was crestfallen. I thought I was a strong mother who had a balanced approach to parenthood. I was fun, right? Wrong. I took a breath and dared inquire to my 18-year-old daughter that night in Dublin what exactly made me a "strict" mother?

"Oh", she said as she sipped her Guinness, her face reddening as she was now put on the spot. "It was the curfew! I mean, 10 pm on a school night and midnight on weekend nights was rough. All of my friends got to stay out way later."
Oh. That. Well, that's a relief.

So that hot August day, in 2013, on my way home from Penn State, when she told me (in writing, no less!) that she knew parenting wasn't easy, and that she loved me with all her heart, and that I was indeed an amazing parent, I was incredulous. A lady at the neighboring gas pump asked me if I was okay. I explained I had just dropped my baby off at college, and she nodded and smiled. I drove home and smiled the whole way, thinking what a brave person I was!

Until I got home... my tiny 1250-square-foot house seemed so incredibly palatial all of a sudden. The dog was the only other soul in the house. I looked at her and said, "What next?" She looked at her leash, then back at me. "Okay," I said, "let's go." And off we went to find out what exactly was next, indeed.

If you have a partner instead of or in addition to a dog, this scenario could play out much differently. You and your partner might walk into the house, and both collapse in tears, or relief! Maybe you've been waiting for this chance to be alone, to take your love in a new direction.

If you're single, you may need to start navigating from what might feel like ground zero. I didn't know who I was if I wasn't mothering. Developing a sense of self takes some self-reflection.

 Jill's correct. Taking the time to develop a sense of self takes self-reflection and the choice to move forward. Here are some of the questions I've asked myself recently to help me create a brighter future for myself:

- What are some of the dreams I had as a little child?
- If money were no object, what would I do and why?
- Do I surround myself with people who encourage me or drain me?
- Am I taking care of my body as I should? What can I do to improve my health?
- Am I in control of my money?
- Have I come to terms with my past and forgiven myself and others?
- Do I accept that I'm getting older and embrace it?
- Can I age safely in my home?
- If I want to develop my spirituality, how will I take that journey?
- Am I spreading love in the world?
- Am I taking the time to connect with the people I love?

Don't be afraid to ask yourself questions like these. People who are thriving throughout their lives often do this. They take a long look in the mirror and examine themselves. From this, they determine what matters to them and get a clearer picture of what they want. Shortly after I turned 50, I received an envelope in the mail from AARP. I laughed and said to myself, "Well, I'm officially old." But the truth is, it's an excellent resource on how you can live a fulfilling life. It's also an excellent resource to help you prepare for life's curveballs.

Remember, I said it was often in your 50s that the crisis hits? For me, it was the passing of my husband and the decline of my mother's and father's health all in the same year. I was literally "sandwiched" in between caring for my dying husband and aging parents and providing for my children and grandchildren. The role of the family caregiver is exhausting! Even if you're an expert at navigating senior care. The fact is it's emotionally and physically exhausting. You must have a plan in place and a Plan B if Plan A isn't working out!

Before anyone agrees to take on the role of the family caregiver, they must examine and give an honest assessment of what they can and can't do for someone. When my husband was first diagnosed with cancer, he didn't need me to help him take a bath; however, as the disease progressed, he became so weak that he couldn't stand steady on his feet. I was no longer strong enough to help lift him in and out of bed and onto the shower chair, and to be honest, I was very nervous about him falling. I just wasn't the best person for the job. I also had a tough time helping him with his feeding tube. It freaked me out. I wasn't equipped to do it. My daughter, on the other hand, was a rock star and nothing seemed to bother her. You really must start with how things will look as your loved one ages and disease progresses.

You need to ask the difficult questions, like:

- What if they can no longer walk?
- What if their memory fades?
- What if they can no longer drive?
- What if they become incontinent?
- What if they can no longer use the stairs?
- What if they can no longer get in and out of bed?

You have to imagine the worst-case scenario and then determine what you'll need to do to care for that. Being honest about what you can and can't do for someone is the best way to love them. It's not going to do anyone any good if you're not physically or emotionally capable of handling the job. Even if you're well equipped to be a caregiver or are a skilled nurse. You still have to sleep. NO ONE CAN DO IT ALONE! There's a reason there are home care agencies, assisted living communities, and nursing homes. Sometimes it's best for your aging loved one to be cared for by a professional.

According to Aginginplace.org, at least 20% of adult children are taking care of an older parent. Here are some statistics from their website:

- Over 40 million family caregivers provided 37 billion hours of care for loved ones in the past five years. The value of this care is estimated at $470 billion.
- About 85% of family caregivers in the U.S. do not receive any respite care.
- The last phase of life is generally 4.5 to 5 years.

- Nearly half of family caregivers over age 40 handle medical tasks, from changing bandages to inserting catheters or feedings tubes. Among that group, only 47% say they have received adequate training to perform those tasks.
- Depression affects 20 to 40% of all caregivers.
- Nearly half of caregivers have trouble balancing work and caregiving.
- Of working caregivers, 8% state that they have been sidelined from job-growth opportunities because of their caregiving responsibilities.
- Half of the adult caregivers say it's moderately or very difficult to balance work and caregiving.
- Three-quarters of the respondents found it stressful, and more than half found it overwhelming.

The statistics also don't give you a behind-the-scenes look into how this emotionally plays out in the family. Families have issues—unresolved anger, guilt, unforgiveness.... Let's face it; families have dysfunction! And the truth be told, many of us don't have the best relationships with our parents and siblings. They're often fractured. And now here it is, "the crisis," the call in the middle of the night from the hospital that Mom has fallen or Dad has had a stroke (and remember, no one ever thought this could happen; your parents were the pillar of health, YESTERDAY). You all rush to the hospital to hear the doctor tell you the bad news that your parent can no longer live independently. They'll need someone to help them with all their activities of daily living (housekeeping, meals, bathing, dressing, medication management) or specialized nursing care. If you've had a strained relationship before this crisis, make sure you don't put on rose-colored glasses now and just assume everyone is going to have Mom's best interest. If your family is already strained, it's best to reach out to a professional like a Senior Advisor or a Patient Advocate who can help.

Even the most loving and supportive families will find it challenging to care for an aging parent. It's an emotional time watching your parents decline in health and knowing that they're coming to the end of their lives. It's especially physically exhausting if you're the family caregiver, and you must be aware that caregiver burnout is a real thing!

Caregiver burnout is a state of physical, mental, and emotional exhaustion. It happens when help isn't available or if a caregiver tries to do more than they have the time, money, or energy to manage.

The early signs of burning out are when you find yourself becoming irritable and strained. You might start to feel angry. You may also feel like you're being pulled in a million different directions as you try to maintain your life and caregiving duties.

Other signs of burnout are:

- withdrawal from friends, family, and other loved ones
- loss of interest in activities you previously enjoyed
- changes in appetite, weight, or both
- changes in sleep patterns
- getting sick more often
- feelings of alienation, helplessness, or hopelessness
- excessive use of alcohol, medications, or sleeping pills
- losing control physically or emotionally
- feeling stressed in the patient's presence
- difficulty concentrating

Don't ignore these warning signs of burnout. They'll only get worse, and what good would you be to the person you're caring for if you end up in the hospital? There's a point at which you must communicate your feelings to your family and doctor.

As your loved one is aging, you have to take the time to continually evaluate the current care plan and be open to making changes in the event their health declines further. Always keep in mind that it's okay to say you're not capable or unable to provide the care they need.

Currently, my sister has chosen to be the full-time caregiver of my mother. She's moved in with my parents and helps my mother with all her activities of daily living. My mother has dementia, and her mobility is declining. My dad, sister, and other siblings spend a lot of time talking about how it's all going. We recognize that as my mother ages and her mental state continues to decline, at some point my sister won't be able to care for my mom anymore. We've already discussed when it would be appropriate to move her into an assisted living or skilled nursing home. My sister also knows that at any time, she's allowed to say she doesn't want to continue caring for Mom. We respect her, support her, and understand that this is a choice she's made, and she's also allowed to end the agreement.

My sister's health and well-being are just as important to me as my mother's. If she, as the caregiver, is no longer thriving, then it's time to do something else. I don't want my sister to become one of the rising statistics of caregivers who are passing away from stress before the person they're caring for does.

Your Home and Your Space

Now you can officially stop saying, "This is why we don't have anything nice." You don't need to keep the well-worn couch anymore unless you LOVE it, of course. You have the power and perhaps the resources to change the look and feel of your home. You can most likely go to a furniture store and upgrade your sofa, dining set, or kitchen table if you'd like. Totally cool, and I'm all for this! All I ask is this:

Don't buy new furniture or big stuff without making sure you have a plan for where the old stuff is going (first)!

So this means that you have to do a little research, pick up the ol' cell phone, and start making arrangements to have your old items picked up by a charitable company or a hauling service if it's genuinely trash. There are several resources in your community that can make this happen, but they need lead time to schedule you. Suppose it's a charitable pickup, like the Vietnam Vets. In that case, they have a separate furniture pickup that comes out, in addition to their other trucks that get dispatched several different times a day to get smaller items, boxes, and bags from people's driveways and front porches.

If you had kids, your kids have most likely moved out by now. If they're still living with you, you either had your children when you were older than your peers, or they're freeloading. Either way, you have some freedom now that you didn't have when caring for them full time. You may want to start the downsizing process NOW. This means making decisions while still really sharp and able to figure out what items in your home complement your current lifestyle. Also, let's be honest—we're physically stronger now than we will be in our 60s. My clients hire me and my team because they can't "do the steps" anymore, nor do they want to climb up and down on those steps carrying heavy objects or make 20 trips on those stairs carrying things piece by piece.

Put One Foot in Front of the Other (But Start Walking NOW)
Where do you begin? My biggest tip is to start with storage spaces (yes, this means going down to the darn basement), which are usually the areas of your home that contain items you've begun to say goodbye to but can't completely sever your relationship with. Yes, yes. It's an overwhelming process. The good news is that you don't have to do it all at once. And you don't have to do it perfectly (isn't that a relief?). Often, procrastination is viewed as being lazy or stuck in some way. Most of the time, however, it's caused by a sense of perfectionism. We do happen to wait, sometimes, for the planets to align before we begin.

This hypothetical but completely realistic situation might look like this:
"I was going to organize my closets as soon as I got a day off," or...
"I'm going to sort through that office as soon as my husband goes away for the weekend—I can't concentrate when he's here."

And then the day off comes, and it's a LOT more fun to shop at the mall, get the car washed, and call your friend (whom you haven't talked to in ages…today's the day!) than it is to get that closet "done." You might also have a parent who needs you to pick them up from the doctor's or get bananas for them because they forgot them at the store today. Or, well, Netflix.

I get it. It's reasonable to want to avoid what could potentially be a difficult day of tough decisions. I usually suggest scheduling it and not the whole day for this project. Make the goal to find 10 items that day you no longer want or use in that space. It doesn't all have to be the same type of thing—it's okay to have something from your junk drawer in the same donation box as your pink umbrella that you never used. As you get better and your routines start including a daily "weeding out," you'll find that you're making significant progress, and who knows, maybe the 10 items can become 20!

Read that Room like a Book
- Collect a few supplies before you start sorting your belongings in any space: small and medium-sized cardboard boxes, garbage bags, a Sharpie, and a rag.
- Write "Donate" on the cardboard boxes, and line a large garbage can with your trash bag. You may want a real trash bag and trash can for true garbage to make sure your second thoughts don't thwart your efforts. To avoid confusion, either keep it far enough away from the bag you're using to donate or use clear bags for trash and black bags for donation items.
- Grab some painter's or masking tape, and put a piece of tape about three feet from the left wall on any surface—that's your finish line.
- Working left to right, top to bottom, take things off of shelves, out of cabinets, off of surfaces, and use the OHIO technique (Only Handle It Once) to decide if you'll keep it, toss it (or recycle it), donate it, or sell it.
- Once you reach your finish line, you can determine if you want to keep going, or if you're going to get those items you said goodbye to where they need to go—a charity, to the consignment store, or set aside for the online auctioneer to review later. When you "read a room," you can see your progress visibility each time you revisit the space to continue. Move the tape, and get going again!

Time Is a Container, Too

When planning to sort and declutter a large space, like a garage, I often hear people say, "I'm going to do my basement this weekend." I advise these people to please start a little smaller, with a more manageable, measurable goal: Sort and declutter five square feet in the morning and the items you want to donate to a charity, containing and labeling the items you want to keep long term. Place a date on the label when you close the lid so the next time you want to edit your belongings, you see when you last reviewed them. It's a lot easier to get organized and take an inventory of the items you love and want around you when it's less daunting, and your expectations are met.

Your Financial and Professional Goals

If you haven't created a retirement plan now, THIS IS THE TIME. It's a requirement unless you plan on working until you're dead. Listen, I don't mind working. I thrive on it, a little. But I want to enjoy some time, too, without having to be anywhere else. I feel like this is best achieved if I'm working less, or not at all, so I can explore hobbies and new cities, visit friends, and catch up with their lives. I know what I need every month to live. But I also know what I need every month to live WELL.

Your career may be something you've settled into by now, or the company you started has reached the goals set forth by you decades ago. If you're getting restless, this is the decade to make the changes so you can have a few more decades of enjoying your re-career decision. Regrets are caused by not acting upon your desires for change and growth and exploring new possibilities.

People will pay you for your talents!

Maybe you can ask yourself: How can I create more revenue to expedite wealth creation?

There are many ways you can create an additional stream of revenue for yourself. You have a lifetime of experience and, at this point, are an expert at something. People will pay you for what you know and for services you can provide to help simplify their lives. Ask yourself these questions to help you uncover your zone of genius:

- What am I naturally good at?
- What do people always come to me for advice on?
- What do I hold any professional certifications in?
- What can I talk about for hours?

Any of these answers could lead you to create an online course, book royalties, a consulting or coaching side hustle, and so much more!

Here are just some other ways you can create additional cash flow:

- dog walking
- house sitting
- Airbnb (rent that extra room in that house you should have downsized from by now!)
- drive for Uber or Lyft
- become a virtual assistant
- affiliate marketing (promoting other people's products and services for a commission)

Just get a bit curious around this idea, what do you desire your "retired" years to look like? You can choose to continue to create wealth now from a place of passion rather than necessity.

You're never too old to step into the world of entrepreneurship. Today the fastest-growing sector in the business world is in the online education space! You carry wisdom and solutions to the world's needs; share your knowledge and why not create a nice stream of revenue.

Your Relationships and Social Life

L   Keep socializing. While raising our children, many of us didn't take the time to stay engaged with our friends. It's time to change that. As you age, it's essential to remain socially connected, just like it's important to eat healthy foods and exercise. Cultivate meaningful friendships that will last the rest of your life. Step out of your comfort zone and join some groups and try a few new hobbies. Don't miss out on anything that gets you excited!

J   The friends I have now are so very different from those I sat with at the lunch table in high school, the ones I drank with in college, or the ones I went to playgroups with when we had our kids. Don't get me wrong; I still keep in touch with people from each of those groups. The friends I have now are the ones that, no matter what, we could pick up right where we left off the last time we spoke. Life happens, and if our friends can join us along the journey while that wonderful life is happening, great! If they can't, they can catch up later. And that's okay, too. The friends I have now are those who truly know me and love me no matter what. They're my biggest champions and my Reality Club presidents when I need them to be. If I ask them what's wrong with me, they'll gently tell me because I want them to. They know it's okay. It's safe. We're all adults now, and I love this part of being in my 50s. For some reason, it's okay to take the filter and throw it away (for the most part) and just be who we are. I don't look at them and wonder why they didn't wear makeup today. I already know—they ran out of time, or they simply didn't care to, just like me. I already know by the tone of their voice if we're going to need just to sit together or if we're going to stir up trouble somewhere.

Let's just say you're a little short on friends, for whatever reason…maybe you're shy or moved a lot for a job. We can also say that you had great friends in college, but they all moved around like you, and you're relegated to seeing them sporadically and seeing their lives evolve mainly on Facebook. It's all good! You can make more friends! How, you ask? I have 18 ways to make a new friend. You can join a:

1. Book club (if you like wine, talking, eating, and reading, in that order)
2. Dinner group (if you like to eat at new places in your town and don't mind sitting with about six to 10 people at a table)

3. Wine tasting group (if you want to learn more about wine, want to become a sommelier, or like to drink wine)
4. Beer-tasting group (if you want to learn more about beer or just like beer)
5. Sewing/quilting/crafty group (if you're going to practice a hobby long forgotten or take time to learn something new)
6. A gym where there are classes (classes are key since you can't really strike up conversations around exercise equipment)
7. Board of directors (if you like long meetings about making decisions)
8. Band (if you play a musical instrument)
9. Choir or singing group (if you like to/can sing)
10. Hiking group (you MUST love long strenuous walks UPHILL and should definitely buy hiking boots)
11. Biking group (you should probably have a bike, for starters, and I hope you have a helmet!)
12. Running group (you just need a good pair of running shoes and to show up on time)
13. Volunteer organization where there are PLENTY of events to work at
14. Church group: ladies auxiliary, men's group, committees abound (you should most likely believe in a God—of your choice—and belong to that particular religion to really understand what's going on)
15. Pet rescue team (you really MUST love dogs, cats, and all sorts of furry little pals, and be okay with seeing not-so-great living conditions for them)
16. Neighborhood civic group (if you want to be a part of the success and direction of the community and like to vote on and discuss stuff; also, if you like folding chairs and powdered creamer)
17. Movie club (if you like watching movies—all sorts—and enjoy discussing films in a bar or coffee shop afterward)
18. Card clubs (do you know HOW to play Bridge? No? It's okay. It's a hard one. Learn! Have fun! Bunko, Texas Hold'em, and much, much more)

Just Google it. Trust me, these activities and options are all out there.

If you married in your younger years, you've defied the odds against you. Congrats! This is the time for you to decide as a couple what the rest of your lives could look like together. If you had some issues in your marriage that you didn't have time to address when raising the kids and having your career in full swing, now is an excellent time to reflect, to heal, and move forward together with a sense of renewal. The rest of your life together is ideally going to be the one you have control over, without distractions and major interruptions, other than becoming grandparents and a few health issues here and there. If you're part of a couple, you'll still need to have your partner's input over what that life will look like, despite making some plans of your own.

If you're single and aren't thinking about a serious relationship, now it's time to design the future with no limits, no one to tell you what you can't do since none of your time is shared with someone else's choices for your time, dreams, the kind of home you want to live in, etc.

Visualization is one of the most powerful mind exercises you can do! Every year I sit down and create a vision board or dream board for my life. Whether you believe it or not, it is a powerful tool in achieving the life you desire. Many of the world's most successful, influential people including Olympic athletes create vision boards and use visualization to improve performance.

Creating the life you desire is more than the stuff you want to have. Your board should focus on how you want to feel! The things you want, the fancy car or dream vacation, are good—and yes, put them on the board—but it's much more powerful to focus on how you want to feel when you achieve these goals! The desire you have to see these things come into your life is what will attract them to you.

Anyone can make a vision board. Grab some old magazines, scissors and glue, and a big poster board, and get started. I like to think about the different areas of my life and what goals I have for each of them.

The areas I focus on are:

- my family and relationships
- my business

Chronological Order

- my home environment
- my health and wellness
- my financial goals
- my social and travel experiences
- my spiritual life and growth

After I fill up my board, I place it in a prominent place in my home, and each day I spend a few moments looking at it and imagining what I'll feel like as each of the experiences and goals come into my life. I close my eyes and see myself in Santorini, Greece, sitting with a glass of wine at a table overlooking the Aegean Sea! I feel the light breeze on my face and smell the sea air! I hear the voices from the nearby market and the chatter of the people as they stroll on by. I then speak out how thankful I am that I'll be able to enjoy this trip.

Creating the board itself can become a wonderful experience. Invite some friends over and talk about your dreams together. Speaking your dreams aloud to each other and even holding one another accountable toward some of your goals is another powerful key to a successful life!

> *I see my folks, they're getting old, and I watch their bodies change*
> *I know they see the same in me, and it makes us both feel strange*
> -Bonnie Raitt, *The Nick of Time*

About Your Parents

While you're starting to recognize your own bones creaking and have been working on decluttering your own life, and if you've been fortunate up until this point to not yet experience the "crisis," it's a good time for you to get a bit nosy and more observant of the aging adults in your life. If it's been physically exhausting for you to clean out the garage and you need an adjustment from the chiropractor afterward, just imagine how much more of a challenge it is for your parents. I've often had adult children tell me that their mom or dad is becoming a hoarder. The piles usually start because they can no longer physically clean out closets or get the trash to the curb. It begins a cycle that they soon get caught in.

Often this happens to seniors who don't have family close by. Their children live out of state and only see them once a year. The children are unaware of their loved ones' struggle because they just hear how "fine, good, wonderful" they are when they call. It doesn't matter how old you get; your mom or dad will not want you to worry about them. There's still that part of them that wants to protect, nurture, and care for you. It's unnatural for them not to worry about you.

When the crisis hits and the kids head in from out of town, most of them tell me they had no idea their parent was in such poor health and that they'd been struggling.

Despite having all this knowledge and being known as an expert in the field, I still wasn't making my plan to leave my "earth suit" with a big smile on my face. I finally began to get curious about why I had avoided this, as most of us do. What I discovered is this. It all boils down to three **Big Fat Lies** we tell ourselves and each other as we move through this thing called life:

Lie number 1: I'm not that old/you're still young
Lie number 2: I have plenty of time/you have plenty of time
Lie number 3: I'm fine/you're fine

These are all lies, and as we get older, the cycle of life will cause us to have to come to the truth and face our mortality. Sadly, most will be blindsided and ill-prepared. We'll often be forced to face this thing head-on called "Aging." At first, Aging may slap us in the face with a phone call from the hospital letting us know one of our parents has fallen or had a stroke. (But not you! You're no dummy; you've picked up this book and gotten curious—how fantastic!)

When I had *my* slap, it hit me on both cheeks at once. My husband had been diagnosed with cancer, and my mother was diagnosed with frontal lobe dementia, all within a matter of weeks. It was a year filled with never-ending doctor appointments, trips in and out of hospitals, rehabs, endless phone calls, and sleepless nights. I was fortunate enough to know how to navigate the healthcare system and could coordinate care in my sleep (remember I'm an expert, at least I thought I was!) But it was time to face the truth and get real. All the knowledge I had acquired as a Senior Advisor over the years didn't prepare me for facing the ticking clock of time. I wished I could stop it and often would just pray that it would at least slow down long enough for me to catch my breath. The three **Big Fat Lies** had been exposed. I had to come to terms with the truth:

#1 Laurean, your mother is now old, and look in the mirror; you're now a grandmother. You're aging now too!

#2 Laurean, your husband has terminal cancer, and he'll pass away soon. His days are numbered, and so are yours! How will you spend your last days together, and what will your life be like when he's gone?

#3 Laurean, your mother and husband are NOT fine. They need help, and you do too; you can't do this alone!

After my husband passed away (and I slept for about two months), I woke up and became serious about making sure I took some concrete steps to ensure I was one of the people who got to the end of my life without regret! But it all starts with recognizing the lies we believe about aging and taking action toward planning to live our life fully. What I've discovered is simple... most of us never think about dying. Heck, most of us don't even think about living, but those who do leave this earth pretty happy!

Almost no one likes to admit they need help.

So, it's time for you to start paying attention and reading in between the lines. The next time you have a family gathering or visit your loved one, pay attention. If you begin to see visible signs, like them struggling to get around or being confused, you probably need to be much more proactive and assess if they're still safe at home.

The following questions can be used to determine whether you, a loved one, or a neighbor, are having difficulty performing everyday activities. The results may reveal whether they can live independently or whether intervention is necessary. Keep these in mind the next time you visit!

Medications
- Are prescriptions not being refilled, resulting in failure to take medication when scheduled?
- Has taking medication become too difficult due to poor memory or confusion? Evidence may include pills taken together that shouldn't be, different pills mixed in a pillbox, or an oversupply or undersupply of medications.
- Have conditions previously under control become acute because the medication isn't being taken correctly?

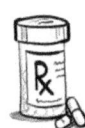

Food and Groceries
- Based on past food habits, are the cupboards frequently empty or being filled with unusual foods?
- Is the food in the refrigerator often spoiled or kept long beyond the "use by" date?

Daily Business
- Is the mail being picked up and opened regularly, or is it remaining uncollected or unopened?
- Are credit cards or checkbooks being misused or not balanced as well as in the past?

Social Contact
- Have social contact occurrences changed significantly, resulting in fewer public outings or limited social visits with close friends?
- Has the ability to drive deteriorated? Is there a fear of driving or a recent history of multiple minor accidents leading to isolation?

Living Habits
- Has there been a change in living habits such as a change in dress or appearance or a decline in personal hygiene not related to physical disability? Is attire appropriate for the weather?
- Have housekeeping habits changed so an ordinarily neat and orderly home is now cluttered and not cleaned regularly?
- Are pets that were usually well cared for suddenly not being fed or cared for as they had been in the past?

Solicitations
- Is there a sudden increase in ordering unnecessary items through the mail or televised advertisements?
- Has there been an increase in calls to family members or healthcare providers?
- Have unnecessary calls been made to 911?

About Your Parents

If you're the adult child of a parent who always hosts for the holidays and they seem just fine with cooking the meal and entertaining everyone at their home, then there's no reason for you to offer to "take it over" from here. Let them guide the conversation. I've heard several women in their 70s say to me that they were really hurt and insulted when their daughters and daughters-in-law commandeered the holiday dinners because they thought it was "too much work for Mom." One of my clients looked very sad when she said, "[My daughters] didn't ask. They just took over, like I didn't even have a say. I hope they don't start thinking for me, too!"

Jill makes an important point. The holidays and family gatherings may now look a little different, but making sure everyone from the youngest to the oldest feels valued and included is critical. The holiday season and other family celebrations are times filled with happy gatherings among our family and friends. They're a time of celebration and joy, a time to remind us all of the brilliant, wonderful things life has bestowed upon us. Unfortunately, for many aging adults, these special times of the year can turn out to be times when joy is replaced by sadness, anxiety, and loneliness, and the holiday blues set in. Let's be a bit more mindful of this.

Here are my top five tips to help beat the holiday blues:

1. Reach out: Social contentedness is especially important at holiday times. Reaching out to older relatives and friends who are alone is something all of us should do.
2. Be inclusive: Involve everyone in holiday preparation, breaking down tasks to include the youngest and oldest family members. (Almost) everyone loves to bake cookies and decorate together.
3. Create new memories: In addition to family traditions, aging adults need new experiences to anticipate. Add something new to the holiday celebration, or volunteer for your family to help others. Enjoy activities that are free, such as taking a drive to look at decorations.
4. Be reasonable with your schedule: Don't overbook yourself into a state of exhaustion—this makes people cranky, irritable, and depressed.
5. Monitor medications and alcohol: If you have senior family members, be sure to help them adhere to their regular schedule of medications during the frenzy of the holidays. Also, pay attention to their alcohol consumption during holiday parties and family gatherings.

LIFE ESSENTIALS:
Things to have in place before you're 59:

- Updated Life Insurance
- Updated Wills
- Updated Living Will
- Updated Vital Records
- Updated Power of Attorney
- Updated Home Inventory (see Life Essentials Chapter)
- Updated Health Benefits
- Updated Care and Living Plan

YOUR SIXTIES

Your Identity and Well-being

I'm sure at this point in your life you're counting down the years, months, days, hours, and minutes 'til you retire. I want to share from my work experience the difference between those who retire and live versus those who retire and exist. You may be very excited to finally punch that last timecard at work, but rest assured, this is a very big change filled with many mixed emotions and a period of adjustment. Many of us just don't go to work, and that's that. For many, we may have worked the same job for 30 years or even more. Our place of employment can also be the place where we made our greatest friends, and it's not just the job we're leaving. When my father retired from working for The New York Times for over 30 years on the night shift, my mother couldn't understand why all he wanted to do was sleep all day. I said, "Mom, he's worked the night shift for over 30 years. His nights *are* his days." To be honest, my dad still would rather sleep all day and stay up all night. It's a big adjustment, and there are going to be times when you'll miss your "working life." You need to acknowledge and prepare for this.

There's a level of fear of the unknown of what's next. The beauty of retirement is that we now have the time and flexibility to do anything our hearts desire. It's also the time we get real about our health and safety as we age. It's time to perhaps consider downsizing from our homes that are way too big and may now become a safety concern for us as we age. It's time to get real with ourselves and not keep avoiding the fact that we're getting older. If you haven't followed the advice of your doctor to shed 20 pounds and are still eating Ding Dongs…well, it's time to stop that and adjust if you're going to have the stamina to travel across the U.S. in an RV. It's also time to sit down with your adult children and have honest conversations about aging. Let them in and let them know what your wishes are.

"…Before I Die," the Invisible Phrase

Speaking of the unknown and considering it heavily as we dive head-in to this decade, most of the people in this age group want to do all those things they didn't do when they were younger, when they didn't have the time or money (or both) to do what they wanted to do. There's this hidden phrase behind those wishes that we sometimes say out loud, but mostly we don't.

"I want to learn how to sail (...before I die)."
"I want to write my novel or memoir (...before I die)."
"I want to hike to the bottom of the Grand Canyon...."

(You get the picture.)

This is the decade where we feel we have to make a lot of stuff happen, and fast, while we still can, while there is time. You may feel this way because it's possible you've developed other physical internal signs of aging, like chronic ailments (high blood pressure, diabetes, and arthritis). You may have more than one or two specialists in your life.

Reminder if you didn't do this!! By the time you're ready to retire, you'd better be sure to appoint someone to be your Power of Attorney and healthcare proxy. This is essential in the event that you're sick and unable to make decisions for yourself. Without these documents, your adult children won't be given access to your health conditions and can't intercede for your well-being. Get it done now!

Okay, so if you haven't seen the signs of aging on your body by now, you will soon! You see photos of yourself taken by a friend, and at first, you say that friend "doesn't know how to take a picture!" Then when you see yourself in a selfie YOU took with your friend a few weeks later, you realize that, indeed, user error wasn't the problem, nor was the lighting or the angle. You actually look old(er)! Ouch. The way I see it, you have three choices:

1. Start clicking on the miracle wrinkle cream ads you used to scroll past on social media.
2. Make inquiries with plastic surgeons just to get your "options."
3. Accept it.

You see signs on restaurant doors that offer senior discounts on Tuesdays, and you find yourself going to those restaurants on Tuesdays. This is okay! This is normal! Hey, the more money you save on that grilled cheese sandwich, the more money you're going to have for that Mediterranean River cruise you have your heart set on!

CHRONOLOGICAL ORDER

Grandchildren and step-grandchildren are wonderful gifts! Speaking of gifts, these same little people LOVE getting gifts from you. Make sure you set a gift budget at the beginning of each year and try not to go overboard in your giving. Getting them a new toy, or game, or computer won't buy their love, but teaching them how to save up for these things is a great legacy to share. (Don't worry, you can still buy them stuff. I'm not totally heartless.)

Simplify! Traditions that always meant so much get boiled down to the most important elements (e.g. simple holiday decorating versus setting up an elaborate Christmas village with a moving locomotive) so the season can be enjoyed without the time it takes to make it "perfect." Don't get me wrong, I LOVE Hallmark Christmas shows. Like a LOT. It's okay to redefine traditions. Make them your own now. Make things easier—not because you're "old now" but because you're beginning to see the commodity of time having so much value and the people around you being so darn important.

This is a time in your life where you may be socializing and traveling more, and going places you only dreamed of as a younger person, when you were working hard and saving your money for this time in your life. I often hear my clients in their 70s and 80s say, "I wish I had gone on more trips when I was more mobile and had energy." Since this book is all about living a simpler, more fulfilling life at every stage and not having regrets, I urge you to travel and even enjoy local excursions at all stages of your lives so you can avoid this feeling.

If you're traveling more, you're leaving your house vacant. This means arranging for pet care, for lawn care and yard maintenance, stopping the mail, arranging for bills to be paid automatically or before you leave, and if you're traveling in the winter and your home is in a cold climate, it means you need to make sure you turn your water of so your pipes don't freeze. Since you're spending more time on the road, in the air, or at sea, your projects will be neglected, and your home, for this decade, may be the last place you attend to in terms of your "stuff."

Photographic Memories: Organizing Vacation Photos

You have a LOT of these by now. I'm going to help you with this. Keep in mind that you and (most of) your family are the only people who remotely care about the trips you've taken unless you're a travel journalist or work for National Geographic Magazine as a contributing photographer. Keeping this in mind, I want, no I **need** you to create a powerful album about your journey as a storyteller you and your loved ones want to know about YOU. *How did YOU experience that trip?* What did you feel when you saw the Mona Lisa for the first time? *What did it feel like* to stand under that waterfall in Bali? Did you get scared when you stood at the top of the Grand Canyon? Who was with you? Why was this trip *so important to you*?

I love photo albums, and I love the new digital books you can make from companies like Shutterfly, MPix, Forever, and Blurb. If you don't have time to create an album, hire a Photo Organizer who specializes in making albums out of your digital photos and can help you sift through the memories painlessly. If all this still sounds like too much work, upload the photos to a digital frame, and enjoy the slide show! My favorite digital frame is Nixplay. It's incredibly easy to use and beautiful to display anywhere in your home—on a surface or mounted on a wall. I love how you can upload pictures easily using apps such as Facebook, Instagram, Google Photos, and Alexa.

> Before you go on your next trip, create a folder in your phone's photo app just for that location or trip. Your phone will time and date stamp those photos, so don't worry about that! Snap away, but just **consciously put those special photos in that folder** every day on your trip. This act alone will help you pick your best vacation photos, which then can be uploaded to your favorite album printing company before you're wheels down on your return home trip. This daily exercise will also help you delete the duds, or the 30 extra sunset pictures so later you have less to declutter out of your phone. Let's be honest...you KNOW when you get home from the trip, you're going to be unpacking and getting organized for your real life within 24 hours of returning, and the trip will just become a distant memory. Your good intentions to make a book or keepsake will get drowned in your everyday life, which is busy enough.

Your Home and Your Space

Unfortunately, this is also the time where you may be pulling more items into your home. An older relative or immediate family member may have to downsize and move, or pass away, and you'll inherit their possessions with the intention of going through them soon, and then...well, you know.... There was that trip to Italy! Then you go to Florida to visit and take care of your sister who broke her hip, and then going on that cruise.... Trips take time to plan and pack for! They take time to transition home from, too. And then you have daily living activities and your normal routines, and voila! You're so far off track from going through that garage full of stuff that you can't seem to get focused on. Now it's become too overwhelming, and you're possibly kicking yourself. This is usually when I get "the call." My clients are now lacking in energy and physical stamina to get through a room full of Aunt Mary's china, collectibles, photos, and assorted decor.

So...why on earth didn't you look at the stuff as soon as you got it? Why didn't you stop it before it even came in your door? I'll tell you why:

- It was too emotional of a time to have to process the feelings that came with touching the item (or truckload of items) you now have in front of you.
- You had your normal everyday life—going to work, watching grandchildren, caring for your parents or other family members, etc.

- You had to take care of your own home.
- You simply didn't want to.
- It was too time-consuming and overwhelming—there's just too much!

All these reasons are legitimate reasons, and they matter.

By the way, this is the age that we typically stop cleaning the house like we used to or attending to the repairs that need to be made. And this, my friends, is when it should be checked and maintained the most. This, my 60-something dear ones, is when you forgot to care about the house, and in 10 years, when you really want to downsize and move, you won't be ready.

The Regret Train has officially pulled into the station, and you're riding in the "If Only" car.

If only you had:

- the house cleaned twice a week to avoid grime formation and buildup (oh, it's building, trust me). "Grime" is the stuff that forms a coating over the dust and dirt that was never removed. Maybe you didn't see it. Vision gets worse as we age. It's not our fault.
- the trees and yard maintained seasonally and annually.
- replaced the old knob and tube wiring in the ceilings of your home periodically, so when the realtor tells you to update your fixtures to stage your home, the wires don't crumble in the handyman's hands (this actually happened to my clients).
- removed the wallpaper (that was so pretty in 1972) and painted that bedroom wall an updated color.
- pulled up the orange shag carpet from 1968 in the basement (after all, it was just a basement!) and updated the flooring in any possible way.
- decluttered the attic of all that baby stuff—clothes, furniture, old strollers—that your daughter or your niece didn't want for her baby (why? who knows—maybe the thought of mice traveling all over it and the amount of dust up there could have turned her off...).

Chronological Order

Downsizing isn't a rumor anymore. You're serious. Decluttering your environment has become a priority. Are you still physically and mentally able to declutter? This is the time to do it.

Your kids have now proven prolifically that they don't want your stuff, as they've established their own homes by now and your stuff isn't in it. They never requested that extra chest with the drawers or the wooden rocking horse (or other nostalgic relics from your childhood) from the attic of your home that you "put aside" for them in 1985. They keep changing the subject somehow or otherwise avoiding you when you remind them of the nice set of glasses you saved for them. (They keep driving away and forgetting them! So weird!) The box of china your mother gave to YOU 20 years ago for you to use that you didn't use but never parted with is something I beg you NOT to shove off on your children (for posterity)! These same children will be calling me saying they inherited a bunch of stuff they didn't need or want from their MOTHER can I help them declutter their home.

 Guilt Trip Tickets for Sale!

Your garage might have items you were given by many people because you had the space to keep it. My home was full of all the stuff *my* mother didn't want anymore, and when I went to move, I had guilty feelings about throwing away a broken Santa sleigh because she sent it to me. I'm sure when my mother put that broken sleigh into the box, she said I could repair it with some Elmer's.

These next questions all depend on the size of your yard, but let me ask you: Do you have $25/week to have the grass cut? How about $50? What about the yard cleanup? Is that easy or hard to do right now? My least favorite thing to find in houses is grime. My least favorite thing to find outside the house is overgrowth. Just like grime is sticky and hard to clean, overgrowth is hard to clean up quickly. It's way easier to maintain a yard regularly for $100 a month in the summer than have a landscaping or tree service come once for $3,000 to clean up the dead brush and layers of leaves from decades of neglect and pull the ivy off the side of the house. If you no longer want to do it, it's okay! Just pay for a service if you'd like to stay in your home longer. If you've experienced denial, no judgment here!

When I moved out of my house in 2019, with a yard I had mowed weekly and two gardens I weeded pretty close to regularly, I still had to pay someone to "clean up my yard" before the photographer came over from the realtor's office. I certainly wasn't going to put my house on the multi-list interwebs looking like it was. I thought it was okay because I was living there. Now that I had to sell it and impress someone else, I was supposed to transform it from its apparent Munster's facade to the cover of Better Homes and Gardens' spring issue (even though it was July) in about a week. No stress there! Unfortunately, the work that goes into getting your home on the market is so daunting that most people put it off, which is completely understandable. The repairs you meant to make a few years ago got put on hold because you needed surgery, and the medical bills were high, or your mom came to live with you, so the cosmetic changes you were going to make to the second floor needed to wait. I chose to go to Ireland for two weeks one year over re-doing my upstairs bathroom. When it came time to sell my house, I had to redo an entire, full bathroom quickly, and I ran into problem after problem while up against a deadline. It (finally) got done, and it looked so good that I almost wanted to stay! I'd been meaning to do that bathroom for YEARS. Every year, though, there was a good reason to not do it:

I didn't have enough money for the project, nor had I saved enough.

- I didn't want to take out a home equity line of credit, either, as I had enough debt as it was.
- I couldn't decide on what colors to use.
- The contractors I called, liked, and trusted couldn't do it when I did have the money.
- There was a bad snowstorm one year, and ice damming actually caused a HOLE in my garage floor, and I could see the basement below. I had to get that fixed, which meant a whole new garage floor. That cost the same as the bathroom remodel.

- The contractors who finally were able to do it were available when I no longer had the money at hand.
- I didn't feel like picking out tile, lighting, a new tub, a new toilet, a sink (what kind?), and a mirror. Too much thinking!
- I was dating a really handy guy who promised to do it for a LONG time and never got to it. This happened twice in 10 years (different guys). "When do you think you'll start?" I would ask. "Soon, baby, soon, don't worry." Sigh.
- I had better things to do, like watch Hallmark and stuff.
- I thought it looked fine the way it was.
- I had to use the money to put a new deck on the house since the old one caved in.

Well, it all got done. Eventually, I sold my house, and I moved on. I LOVED apartment living! I called the maintenance person, and he came up right away to handle anything that leaked or broke! It's amazing. And it's all covered in the rent payment. I didn't have to shovel, scrape ice (because there's a big parking garage attached to the building), or maintain the big yards anymore. I felt safe and secure, and I downsized my possessions so what I moved with me is truly all I own. I made another big change. My fiancé and I made a decision to have someone help us clean twice a month and another person help us walk the dogs due to our work and travel schedules. The money we spend on these services is well worth sacrificing the money we would spend on new clothes and big dinners out because our lives got a lot easier as a result.

My clients have often told me they called me to help them downsize and move because their homes, all of a sudden, seemed like "too much work" or too much trouble to maintain, and they simply didn't want to work that hard anymore. Huzzah! This feeling can happen earlier than the phase of life you're in now, or it can happen much later. This is a personal observation, one you need to make on your own. There may be pieces of the work you don't mind doing (like gardening, for example), but cutting the grass and doing the bigger, more laborious work is no longer rewarding or "exhilarating" like it used to be. Please don't hurt yourself out of pride and the desire to prove that you can still "do it all."

Your family and friends need you too much the way you are (healthy) and have no desire to visit you in the hospital because you fell while cleaning the gutters. These people want to visit you wherever you're living, even if it's not the house you always had. It could be a really nice 55+ community with a TON of great events and activities you enjoy! It could be an apartment building with some amenities that are important to you. If you had children, they want you to be happy and safe, too, just the way you want them to be happy and safe in their lives. They're not going to begrudge you the opportunity to move forward, and usually, the one who holds you back the most is, well, you.

"The kids had all their Christmases here!"
"This is where we brought the babies home from the hospital and where they had their first steps."
"I cooked all our meals in THIS kitchen."
"I slept in this room with my spouse for 35 years."
"I fixed up cars in this garage every Sunday."
"My neighbors are so nice here."

All good reasons to stay.

It's time to make a change in your environment when you spend more of your time managing your stuff instead of your interests.

I've always called my organizing and downsizing business a lifestyle service because our professional team wants people to restyle their lives to be better and simpler, easier, and more enjoyable! It's so important to us to help those individuals who want to stop doing all the tasks that are keeping them from being happy and feeling like they're not living their best life.

It truly is all about the lifestyle you want to live going forward. Jill and I use the term "aging in place" often. This term usually applies when making the home you currently live in more manageable, safe, and organized for your physical needs as you age. Ideally, it could be the home you want to spend the rest of your life in, so your current home may not be suitable for this purpose. If you intend to purchase another home to age in place, then here are the essentials to take into consideration before you sign on the dotted line.

Location, Location, Location
Like with any move, where you live is vital to your happiness and well-being. Here are some factors to consider when choosing a location:

- Cost of living: Different parts of the country are much more affordable than others and worth looking into if you're open to moving to another location.
- Proximity to healthcare: This may not seem like a big concern, but it certainly is. As you get older, trips to doctors and specialists become more and more frequent. You may have always dreamed of living out in the country, but take into consideration you may be traveling often into town. Also, the quality of care and access to additional services you may need, such as a physical therapist, is just as vital.
- Age-friendly community: Does the community have an active aging population with services and programs for its aging population? What kind of supportive services are available as you age, like transportation and meal delivery?
- Climate and weather: Let's face it, even at age 50, shoveling snow can be exhausting. It may be time to take into account moving to a warmer climate or at least into a community that's maintenance-free!
- Staying connected: Consider moving closer to your adult children or POA. I like to say, live closer to the folks who'll show up in a crisis and visit often when you're in the hospital. Staying connected and engaged with those we most love is vital!!

House Features:
When purchasing that next home, be sure to make certain it meets all your needs now as well as when you're 90. Here are features to consider as you begin your search:

- One-story living: Remember, we want to avoid falls! This includes entryways with no steps and a level driveway and walkway!
- Extra-wide doorways and hallways: a 36"-wide doorway makes the house easily accessible for a wheelchair if needed; wide hallways and entryways make for easy navigation.
- Lower-level counters, cabinets, sinks, and sturdy drawers in the kitchen, a stove with controls in the front, so you're not struggling to reach over hot burners
- Lower windowsills
- Lever doorknobs and handles throughout—easier to use even if your hands are arthritic
- Front loading washer and dryers
- Raised electrical outlets, so you don't have to bend over
- No-step entry tiled shower stall with grab bars and handheld sprayer
- Low-maintenance landscaping or hardscaping features in the yard

> Hardscaping refers to hard landscaping materials incorporated into a landscape. This can include paved areas, driveways, retaining walls, sleeper walls, stairs, walkways, and any other landscaping made up of hard wearing materials such as wood, stone, and concrete.

Jill and I have both taken the leap already and downsized from the big homes where we raised our families. We've done this earlier than most, probably because we've had the experience of seeing the struggle for many to maintain their homes as they age and the overwhelm and worry it can cause their adult children. Trust me, I know it can be hard letting go…. but sometimes, the circumstances of your life dictate you need to move. I've found this move to be one of the best decisions of my life.

I reduced my monthly expenses to almost half, and it only takes me about an hour to clean my whole place—I love it! I'm also free of so much clutter. I only kept what I loved, and I feel like I can breathe better. I have the room now to enjoy this next phase of my life.

About Your Parents
It may no longer be safe for your parents to stay in their home. If you're finding you're worried about Mom going up and down the stairs, or she's become more forgetful and keeps leaving the stove on, then now is a good time to educate yourself on the different housing options for your aging parents, who may be in need of some support by now. There's a broad array of options in senior housing, from staying in your own home to specialized facilities that provide 'round-the-clock nursing care. The names of the different types of housing options can sometimes be confusing. We delve further into these many choices in our Life Essentials section at the end of this book. See "Life Essentials: Care and Living Plan".

I know there's a lot to think about when taking into consideration moving your mom or dad into a community—or when you're ready yourself. There are many options and factors in the decision-making process. Every family has their own circumstances and preferences. Many times, families have asked me, "If this was for your mom or dad, what community would you move them to?" My answer is always the same: "My parents aren't your parents. They have different care needs, financially are in a different place, and their interests and hobbies are nothing like what your parents would enjoy." It's different for everyone. Unless a crisis dictates a rapid move, take your time, and have fun on the tours. The communities love to have you and will often invite you to have lunch or join them at an event. You should visit a minimum of three options before making a move. You'll know which place is the best for your family!

Your Financial and Professional Goals

What if I don't have the money to pay for my loved one's care?

If your parent is in need of care and they don't have the resources, you should first reach out to your Local Area Agency on Aging to see what services or programs may help support them. They may be eligible for home care services that may help them remain safely in their home. Your local Area Agency on Aging is an excellent resource and provides information on housing, transplantation, recreation, meal delivery, and how to apply for benefits. They'll also have a care manager come out and do an assessment to determine the level of support your loved one may need. To find your local Area Agency on Aging, go to https://eldercare.acl.gov/.

If their needs are beyond that scope of care to remain at home, or a doctor has determined that they're now in need of skilled nursing care, it's time to apply for Medicaid. Medicaid will pay for long-term skilled nursing care if you meet the income eligibility.

If your parents have been privately paying for care and you're concerned that they may outlive their resources, then YOU MUST get educated on the Medicaid SPEND-DOWN. We also strongly encourage you to meet with a reputable elder law attorney.

What is a Medicaid spend-down?
A Medicaid spend-down is a financial strategy used when an individual's income is too high to qualify for Medicaid. To qualify for Medicaid, individuals often must first complete an income or asset spend-down. That means some of the individual's income or assets must be spent, generally on healthcare and medical-related costs. But you could also spend money on debt, such as a mortgage, a vehicle, or credit card balances.

Some examples of healthcare costs that you might put toward a Medicaid spend-down include:

- medical bills, past and current
- transportation services to get medical care
- home improvements to help with medical care, like a chairlift
- medical expenses, such as eyeglasses or a hearing aid

Every state has a different asset limit required for an individual to obtain Medicaid benefits. The individual would spend down all eligible assets needed to be eligible to receive benefits. Generally, your home and car are considered non-countable assets. Keep in mind, if you own a second home or have investment properties, they'll more than likely be counted as a countable asset and will need to be sold, with the money going toward healthcare expenses.

IRAs and 401(k)s are considered countable assets unless you're already receiving your monthly payout. Investments, like mutual funds and stocks and bonds, are also considered countable assets. These are all items you need to take into account, and a good estate planner will help you.

Keep in mind the Medicaid spend-down has many factors and varies from state to state; it also factors in married couples. The spend-down program may also be referred to as a medically needy program or Medicaid's Excess Income Program. Contact your local Medicaid office to learn if a spend-down program is available in your state and the rules for applying.

Trusts, such as Miller Trusts and Supplemental Needs Trusts or Special Needs Trusts, are available in some states to help you become Medicaid-eligible. Trusts allow people with disabilities and income or assets higher than Medicaid eligibility guidelines to place a portion of their income or assets into the trust, where it won't be counted. Rules about how these trusts work vary greatly by state. For more information, contact your local Medicaid office or an elder law attorney. Some states offer a Medicaid Buy-In program, which allows people who are under 65 and have a disability to work (as little as one hour per month) and still receive Medicaid benefits.

Your Relationships and Social Life

This is the decade you told yourself you'd slow down, travel more, and retire from a full-time career. Not everyone fully retires, but most people want to. There are those who seem to have more problems retiring because so much of their identity is in their careers. Others seem to have fewer problems, as their identities were more balanced with their work, social groups, kids, neighbors, etc. Figuring out what you can afford, what your financial boundaries are, and how you want to live your "golden years" have become accelerated and sometimes pervasive thoughts.

This is the time to ESTABLISH a solid social calendar before you retire so when you do, you'll have a thriving and jiving lifestyle built on familiar and fun activities you really enjoy.

If you're married, you can now start really planning on fulfilling the goals you once only dreamed about when you were both younger with a lot more constraints on your time. In fact, you can act like kids again if you want! Remember the days when you were planning your future before the busy years kicked in? It was fun to think about all the trips and adventures you could go on together. You can make them happen now! Once the kids are grown and gone, or you have more time, it's easy to fall into a rut, which is a slippery slope, my friends. Ruts are really just routines gone sour and lifeless. Unhealthy routines turn into bad habits. How many hours per day are you watching TV? Did you read the newspaper, eat, then nap, then read some more stuff online, then nap, then eat, then watch a show, then snack and watch the news? Time for bed! Where did the day go?

There's nothing wrong with hanging out around the house—nope, not at all. The trouble comes when we have about 20 years of this activity, and we're not challenging ourselves to fulfill the goals and dreams we once had when we would have the time to do them. The other negative part of having a daily rut is that your active partner wants you to join him or her for that walk, that trip, or that cool wine-tasting adventure, and if you continue to not join in, you can be hurting the relationship. Most of those things, if not all of them, are within reach now.

It's all possible now, and even more so once you stop working full time. Put pen to paper and get planning:

What do you want to do?

Where do you want to go?

Who do you want to spend more time with or visit?

If you're NOT married, dating in your 60s can be a lot of fun! You don't need each other's incomes and can enjoy each other and make fun plans. There are no mutual financial burdens you each have. College loans are LONG gone unless you went back to school in your 40s (which is okay! The purpose of dating isn't to get married and have children. It's just to have fun!).

However, if you do decide to get married in your 60s, which I'm all for, just make sure you protect your assets and the financial gifts you want to share with your loved ones when you die (or worse if you divorce). There are so many missing conversations in this area because, of course, they're uncomfortable. When people arrange for prenuptial agreements, it can feel offensive at first, and there can be a lot of contention surrounding the entire act. I would offer that if it feels a little awkward now, it will feel a LOT more uncomfortable when there's a death or divorce, and the legal language that was never spoken or included will now adversely affect all involved.

"Prenups" are actually healthy to consider because drawing one up lets you BOTH determine how you want property divided and how you want retirement savings and benefits distributed, without relying on the default legal terms of the state.

Your family may be large by now, and your adult children, blended families, and extended families are pulling you in one happy direction, while your aging parents are pulling you in another, more worrisome direction. You may no longer be hosting the holiday dinners anymore but are traveling to a niece's house, a son's house, and so forth because that is just "easier for everyone."

LIFE ESSENTIALS
Things to have in place before you're 69:

- Updated Life Insurance
- Updated Wills
- Updated Living Will
- Updated Vital Records
- Updated Power of Attorney
- Updated Home Inventory
- Updated Health Benefits (see Life Essentials Chapter)
- Updated Care and Living Plan

YOUR SEVENTIES

Your Identity and Well-being

You're still capable. Your age doesn't have to limit your abilities.

Unless you're super healthy, you're spending a portion of your month visiting a doctor or a lab to get blood work so you can go back to the doctor. You should also have annual physicals to make sure you're doing everything you can to stay well and also staying ahead of anything that might threaten your health. Your lungs get a nice pulmonary test, your ears get a good listening to, and your heart is given a nice once over. Annual physicals help you know your stats, and I'm all for awareness! I love finding out if my blood pressure is still where I want it, or my cholesterol levels are still "within normal limits." I also really like physicals because they give me a chance to see the results of the changes I've made since last year's physical. I love goals, and moreover, I love achieving those goals. Sometimes you get news you don't want like your hearing test didn't go so well in the left ear. Or your blood work shows some concerns. If you're getting annual physicals, then you're within a year of developing symptoms of whatever's wrong with you, so there's usually a good chance you can put together a plan to make yourself healthier. People who blow off this important checkup are really at risk.

It's a good time to review cognitive skills, too, and look at the normal signs of aging versus more brain-based disorders like Alzheimer's and dementia.

One of the best advances I've seen in the newer insurance plans is that they're getting more proactive each year. The insurance company is doing this mostly because they want to pay less in claims, but I don't care what their motivation is—I just care about yours. People don't read the fine print, but most benefit plans today—yes, including Medicare offer so many incredible options from gym memberships and classes about nutrition to medication management. These are all included with your monthly premiums and are usually well worth the time and effort it takes to sign up and get involved. Besides, you could make some new friends, and maybe start a new walking or biking group in the process. How cool is that?

Now that your fridge and pantry aren't being raided by teenagers or starving college kids, this is a great time to reevaluate your nutrition. It is still really crucial to **feed your longevity, so let's talk about some healthy options, that are also convenient to keep on hand.**

Fruit
Fresh fruit is portable and easy to keep around. It can be kept fresher longer - up to 3 days longer - by washing it when you arrive home with a vegetable and fruit wash. Frozen fruit is great to throw in a blender along with some milk and honey, for a delicious smoothie.

Vegetables
Shopping the perimeter of your grocery store is the best way to stay healthy and have fresh choices for your produce, which should include vegetables like broccoli, spinach, cucumber, salad greens, and seasonal goodies like squash, zucchini and sweet potatoes.

Cheese
Hard cheese is great, but soft cheese like cream cheese and cottage cheese make great mixers for fruit, cracker toppings, and snacks. Cottage cheese provides protein plus calcium, two really important parts of a healthy mean plan.

Nuts
Almonds, walnuts, cashews - these are great to keep in the car or your purse for quick snacking that will fill you up and give you some protein and fiber along the way. If you can get used to unsalted, that is a much healthier option.

The clock is ticking, and it's imperative that you have a plan in place in the event of an emergency. Don't assume your children can care for you or that you can stay in your house for the rest of your life. Not everyone is a caregiver, and they just may not be equipped to help you—and that's okay!

The one concern I see and hear over and over from the many aging clients I've helped is that they don't want their kids to worry. Sadly, most of us will keep our struggles to ourselves and don't seek the support of our families because "they're busy." Most aging adults feel they'll be a burden on their children, and they're not honest about how they really are. When the out-of-state daughter calls and asks how they're doing, they just reply "great" or "fine." Their children have no idea that they're now having a hard time mowing the lawn, cleaning the bathroom, and mopping the floor. It's time you take the initiative and get real about what limitations you may have now or in the future and work with your family to find the best solution for you as you continue to age. It may no longer be safe for you to remain in your home, and you may now find it's getting harder to maintain that big house.

On the flip side of that are the thousands of adult children who've called me concerned about their parents but are fearful of having an adult conversation about aging. They worry that their parents will be mad at them or are afraid they'll be perceived that they're trying to tell their mom or dad what to do. There are a lot of family dynamics at play here, but the truth is you need to have healthy conversations that are open and honest. It's time to evaluate and consider your options. Be flexible and open to new ideas. Let your kids in and plan so you can continue to thrive safely.

Speaking of safety, the two most common reasons an aging adult ends up in the emergency room can be prevented with some organization and mindfulness. Let's talk about them while we're on the subject of checking in on our aging loved ones. Here they are:

Falls

Falls and accidents seldom "just happen." The more you take care of your overall health and well-being, the more likely you'll be to lower your chances of falling. Here are a few tips to keep you upright!

- Keep your home well-lit inside and out. Make sure there's good lighting with light switches at the top and bottom of the stairs.
- Keep your hallways and pathways free from clutter.
- Make sure all carpets are fixed firmly to the floor so they won't slip. Add no-slip strips on tile and wooden floors.
- Have handrails on both sides of all stairs—from top to bottom
- Mount grab bars near toilets and on both the inside and outside of your tub and shower.
- Place non-skid mats on all surfaces that may get wet.
- At night use nightlights in your bedroom and bathroom.
- Keep your telephone near your bed.
- Keep electric cords and telephone wires near walls and away from walking paths.
- Arrange your furniture and other objects so they're not in your way when you walk.
- Make sure you can navigate getting in and out of bed, chairs, and sofa safely. You may need to adjust the height.
- Keep moving. Regular exercise helps keep you strong and improves muscle tone.
- Have your vision and hearing tested often. Slight changes in sight and hearing can make you less stable.
- Know the side effects of any medication you're taking. Some may cause dizziness or drowsiness, which could lead to a fall.

Mismanagement of Medication

The Center for Disease Control reports that up to 50% of prescribed medications are *"taken incorrectly, particularly with regard to timing, dosage, frequency, and duration."* This can be fatal, especially for the elderly, whose health sometimes relies on taking the correct medications at the correct time. One of my clients thought she'd forgotten to take her

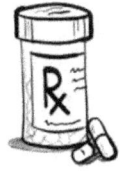

medication and ended up double dosing on her blood pressure medication, causing her to get dizzy. She ended up falling and fracturing her hip. She never regained full mobility and had to move from the home she loved into an assisted living community.

As you get older, you not only have a primary care physician who may prescribe medication, but you also may have specialists like cardiologists, neurologists, and others who also may be prescribing daily medications. It's vital that you have a written list with you, at all times, of your current prescriptions and present them each time at your appointments. Whenever you get any new prescriptions or changes to dosage, be sure to have your pharmacist look over everything as well! Again, you can't assume they're all making sure that these medications are correct and safe to be taken together.

Here are tips to safely manage your medications:

Compile a List of Medications and Make a Schedule
Keep a copy with you at all times. Be sure to include the following information:

- the name of the medication
- what the medication treats
- the frequency that you need to take the medication
- how often the medication needs to be refilled
- the side effects of the medication

My friend recently traveled with her husband and two other couples on a vacation out of the country that was led by a professional tour group. During the trip, one of the women became ill and sought emergency medical attention at a hospital. The ER doctor asked the husband of the sick woman what medications she was taking. He said he had them all memorized and then promptly couldn't produce the right list of subscribed pills she took every day. He was stressed, scared, and exhausted, and his memory wasn't at its best in normal situations. My friend asked him if he kept them written down in his wallet, and he said he didn't need to; he knew he would remember. He finally stated that he remembered and gave the doctor the wrong medicine list from his memory. If my friend hadn't been there to know what the names of the pills were and what they were for, and actually hadn't spoken up, there could have been more of a medical emergency than they were in already. When they returned home, my friend shared with me that he and his wife wrote down all their prescriptions and dosages on a small sheet of paper and put them in each other's wallets.

There many apps, online programs, and binder kits you can purchase to organize this information easily. In case of an emergency, just pull up the information. If you're single, make sure your emergency contact or Power of Attorney has this information handy and can share it easily. It could save your life and help first responders when they're performing triage.

Ask Questions

Don't be afraid to ask questions about the medication your doctor is prescribing to you. This is your body and health. Here are some concerns you may have that you should never be afraid to ask your doctor or pharmacist about:

- How do I take this medication? (Not every prescription comes in pill form.)
- How often do I take this?
- What are the potential side effects?
- Should I take this with food?
- How does this react with the other prescriptions I'm taking?
- What happens if I miss a dose?Can I drink alcohol while on this?

Maintain One Pharmacist

You should do your best to limit yourself to one pharmacist. This way, they know the range of medications you're taking and your medical information while understanding how all the drugs prescribed by varying doctors can affect you.

I'll admit I have no idea how anyone can manage all their prescriptions. I have a hard enough time remembering to take a 10-day supply of antibiotics, let alone numerous pills several times a day. When my husband was dying, we utilized a service that helped keep his prescriptions in order for us. His medications came already separated by time of day in a convenient package. Ask your pharmacist if they provide any similar service. If not, here are some options to consider as well.

Products and Services to Help

PillPack

This full-service pharmacy service does all your management for you because all you have to do is open the packages they send you and take the medication. It cuts out visits to the pharmacy and the process of sorting your medication. PillPack handles everything for you, including refills, all shipped right to your door. All that's needed to get started is the list of your medications, your doctor's information, any insurance information, and your payment method.

MedaCube
This device was designed for those who are struggling to take their medications. MedaCube can dispense up to 90-day supplies of 16 different medications. Each bin is then assigned a time that it needs to be taken. When it's time to take the medication, the device beeps and dispenses the pills.

CYCO smart pillbox
Like other products on this list, Qualife's CYCO pillbox aims to help the elderly with their medication adherence. A dual sensor with visual and audio aids helps ensure that the correct pills with the proper dosages are consumed at the appropriate time.

One day, you will die.

Just as the sun rises and sets each day, sometime, sooner or later, we all must die. This is one of life's certainties. There's often a lot of fear around the subject of death. For some, they're still carrying grief and sorrow from a lost loved one, and the thought of talking about their own life ending is just too painful. For others, there's a concern for family and friends they'll leave behind.

As difficult as this may be for you to talk about, it's important that your family knows your wishes. This will make it much easier for them to honor you after you've passed on. An excellent free resource online to help you and your family get comfortable with talking about the end of life is The Conversation Project (www.theconversationproject.org). Their website has many helpful tips and articles to guide you. They even have a free downloadable conversation starter kit! We provide much more information about this topic in our **Life Essentials** section at the end of this book. See **Wills** and **Living Wills**.

This is probably a good time to also educate you on hospice care. Since you've now reached your 70s, I know you may be aware by now of what this is and what it isn't! There are many misconceptions about hospice, and I've found that this is the most underutilized FREE benefit we're all entitled to. In fact, many families are unaware of all the services it provides for them from which they could have benefited.

What is hospice? Hospice is about death but also about providing quality of life! It's about keeping the patient and family at the center of the caregiving circle. It's care and support for all: the patient, family, friends, and the health professional community.

The care provided isn't meant to cure but to help relieve and reduce discomfort. This care is often referred to as palliative care. Typically, if a doctor certifies that a person's life expectancy is six months or less, they're eligible. However, some who have debilitating diseases like Alzheimer's and Parkinson's may be eligible for hospice care for much longer.

Services included in hospice care:

- medical and nursing care
- medical equipment (hospital beds, walkers, oxygen, wheelchairs)
- pharmaceutical services
- medication
- pain management
- social workers
- home health aides
- home care aides
- dietitians
- therapists, clergy
- bereavement services
- pet therapy
- volunteers
- and more!

In 1982, Congress enacted the Hospice Benefit under Medicare. Hospice services are fully covered under Medicare. Hospice care can be provided in your home, assisted-living community, nursing home, or hospital.

When my husband died, we couldn't have managed without the guidance of our hospice team. They helped us coordinate everything Bill needed. From medical supplies and equipment, delivery of medications, and home care providers who helped him shower and dress to visits from clergy and volunteers just to brighten his day and give us a much-needed rest. For over a year after he passed away, I also received phone calls, cards, text messages, and grief counseling support for my kids. Our hospice team helped advocate for his care when we had to move him into the nursing home, and they helped coordinate that move. They truly helped us focus on what was most important and gave us the time to do it.

Please reach out to your healthcare provider or hospital social worker and learn more about the hospice providers in your area. When it's needed, bring in the help so you can free up your to-do list and be present in the moments you have left together with your loved one!

What I've observed is that the aging adults who are thriving are honest about their limitations and seek ways to remain engaged and active despite any health limitations they may have. They continue to remain a vital part of the community and often volunteer and give back to others. Just because they're retired doesn't mean they're living alone and isolated in their homes. However, on the flip side of this, there are those who are not being honest about the changes that are happening to them. One of the biggest issues of denial is loss of memory.

Let's talk a bit here about "forgetfulness." Each of us, no matter how old we are, experience periods of forgetfulness. Misplacing our car keys or forgetting to grab milk from the store, or paying a bill on time…. It happens! Usually, it's because we have way too much on our to-do lists and have simply forgotten because our minds are busy with 10 other things. Forgetfulness also manifests more frequently when we're not taking proper care of ourselves by staying up too late, not drinking enough water, and eating poorly. Stress is also a cause of forgetfulness. We refer to this as normal forgetfulness. All these causes can be reversed by making ourselves a priority.

Many families will often miss the early warning signs of potentially serious memory loss. Many will be in denial of the issue or simply just say, "Well, they're getting older, so that's the way it is." The fact is many people do age well into their 90s with their minds sharp as a tack. However, be aware of the early signs. Early intervention is key to understanding and preparing for what may be ahead. Here's what the National Institute on Aging says in regard to what's normal and what signs to look for:

What's Normal Forgetfulness and What's Not?
What's the difference between normal, age-related forgetfulness and a serious memory problem? Serious memory problems make it hard to do everyday things like driving and shopping. Signs may include:

- asking the same questions over and over again
- getting lost in familiar places
- not being able to follow instructions
- becoming confused about time, people, and places

Mild Cognitive Impairment
Some older adults have a condition called mild cognitive impairment, or MCI, in which they have more memory or other thinking problems than other people their age. People with MCI can take care of themselves and do their normal activities. MCI may be an early sign of Alzheimer's, but not everyone with MCI will develop Alzheimer's disease.

Signs of MCI include:

- losing things often
- forgetting to go to important events or appointments
- having more trouble coming up with desired words than other people of the same age

If you have MCI, visit your doctor every six to 12 months to see if you have any changes in memory and other thinking skills over time. There may be things you can do to maintain your memory and mental skills. No medications have been approved to treat MCI.

Dementia and Aging
Dementia is the loss of cognitive functioning—thinking, remembering, learning, and reasoning—and behavioral abilities to such an extent that it interferes with daily life and activities. Memory loss, though common, isn't the only sign. A person may also have problems with language skills, visual perception, or paying attention. Some people have personality changes. *Dementia isn't a normal part of aging.*

There are different forms of dementia. Alzheimer's disease is the most common form in people over 65.

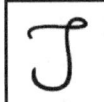 Here's what Rachel Wonderlin, Dementia Care Consultant and Author of *When Someone You Know Is Living in A Dementia Care Community* and *Creative Engagement: A Handbook of Activities for People with Dementia* (A Johns Hopkins Press Health Book) says in a recent blog post:

> *"Dementia is an umbrella term for a group of symptoms of cognitive loss. These symptoms are caused by many different diseases. What does that mean? I like to explain it this way: if you go to the doctor, and the doctor says you have cancer, you'd probably ask, "What type of cancer is it?" You wouldn't leave the doctor without finding out this information. We want to treat dementia the same way: we want to find out what cause or form of dementia a loved one has!*
>
> *Like cancer, dementia is an umbrella term. Saying "Alzheimer's and dementia" in the same sentence is like saying, "Skin cancer and cancer." Everyone knows that skin cancer is a form of cancer, but, for some reason, people think that Alzheimer's is a totally different thing than dementia. It's not. Alzheimer's is a type of dementia."*

Remember, Alzheimer's disease is just one cause of dementia. There are currently over 70 types of dementia, and Alzheimer's is the most common. The most common types of dementia are:

- Alzheimer's disease
- Vascular dementia
- Lewey body dementia
- Frontotemporal dementia
- Mixed dementia

If you or a loved one have been diagnosed with dementia, Alzheimer's, or any other progressive disease, YOU MUST TAKE CARE OF ALL THE LIFE ESSENTIALS ASAP!!

Chronological Order

With any dementia diagnosis, we must be even more proactive and aware of the challenges they present. I've said it's often the "unseen" disease; many times, people are fit physically, but their minds are slipping. Family and friends may not see the signs right away. Often doctors even miss the signs because their patients come in and are having a lucid day and are able to answer all the questions, but a few hours later, they can't tell you the time of day. Families don't notice because Mom seems fine when they visit, but then you start to notice she's losing weight, and it's then you realize she isn't remembering to eat because the food you brought her last week is still in the refrigerator. The clues start to appear: the unopened mail, and she's still in her PJs at 3 P.M. It begins to rear its ugly head.

At some point, one person can't physically care for someone with dementia on their own. That someone will often need 24/7 care as their cognitive ability declines. The disease is horrible. At first, they may just need friendly reminders and can still be socially okay. Eventually, they'll no longer remember who you are and can no longer feed, bathe, or dress themselves. They may also "sundown"—a term for them confusing day and night or not sleeping at all at night any longer. They also may become at risk of wandering. The confusion may bring them back in their memory to a time when they still had a job, and they may wake up in the middle of the night and get dressed and leave the home or try to drive the car. They may now need a secure memory care community to keep them safe.

Safety and well-being for you and your family are now the primary concern as this disease progresses. You need to educate yourself early on care communities and let go of the guilt and promises that you'll care for your loved one forever. You can only do what you can do! You have to know your limitations and let go of expectations. It's all about the best care plan, not about promises you made when you had no idea of what was coming. The best promise we can make to each other is, "I will always do what's best for you, no matter how I feel about it!"

Your Home and Your Space

You've most likely left your larger home and are living in a smaller home by now, since the idea of living more simply may be more desirable, as caring for and maintaining the house might be more physically challenging (and exhausting!). If you haven't yet done your big transition into the smaller space, then this is the decade of your life in which you'll most likely do it!

If you have decided to "age in place" instead of transitioning, so many things can be done to adapt your existing home to increase convenience and safety.

Lowering cabinets, widening doorways, and replacing carpet with tile, wood, or laminate flooring are all ways to make it easier to maneuver and have access to sinks, food, and every day items in your kitchen and living spaces.

You can change where you "live", or spend the most time, in your home. Using this approach, second floors can be used primarily for guests and storage, and first floors can be converted to include a bedroom and expanded bathroom if they don't already. Bathrooms can be made larger, and step-in showers can be installed to replace traditional bathtubs. Grab bars do not have to be silver and institutional in appearance. Sleek, modern designs can be implemented, and many tools that have safety in mind can be concealed in stylish ways.

Consult an architect that specializes in Universal Design. According to the National Disability Authority, "Universal Design is the design and composition of an environment so that it can be accessed, understood and used to the greatest extent possible by all people regardless of their age, size, ability or disability. An environment (or any building, product, or service in that environment) should be designed to meet the needs of all people who wish to use it."

One of my clients in Pittsburgh spent a lot of time planning and working with an architect and builder, and completely renovated their home for the purpose of aging in place. We came in and packed up all of the items that would go to storage prior to the work. They changed the home to accommodate their needs, and flow of their activities in their retired lives. The outcome was incredible, and when we unpacked the boxes into the "new" home, everything made sense to them.

The National Aging in Place Council (NAIPC) has developed a great tool on their website (www.ageinplace.org), free of charge, to help you decide how you would like to live at home safely for as long as possible. They address the areas of housing, health and wellness, personal finance, transportation, community, social interaction, and education and entertainment. The guide is extremely helpful for narrowing down what your priorities are in terms of your environment and how you want to spend your time. It helps you determine how important it is for you to have access to medical treatment, the gym, friends, and shopping independently.

Chronological Order

If you're not currently traveling the world for whatever reasons, you may have more time now to look at and enjoy your memorabilia and photos.

Photographic Memories

If you're like most people who breathe in and out, you have pictures. You have pictures of your family, your friends, your pets, your house, events, and vacations. You also have them EVERYWHERE. They're on your computer, on your phone, on those tiny little camera cards that are the size of a quarter, on CDs, and in shoeboxes.

They're in old albums, new albums, and in frames. I understand, and it's normal. However, if you're feeling overwhelmed and you want to get them in order, start by gathering them all together in ONE place. A dining room table is a great place since it has a large surface. Get some index cards and a pen or Sharpie. Write decades at the top of each card: "1950s," "1960s," etc. Spread these cards horizontally on the longest side of your table. Now take a stack of photos or albums (or slides—I know, it will be okay) and place them in the corresponding decade. When you get to the CDs and flash drives, if they have labels, place them right next to those loose photos from the 90s. If they're not labeled, place them in a container or basket next to your computer for further investigation. Once you've gotten your photos in their correct decade, take some shoeboxes and place each decade in a box. If it doesn't fill the box, it's alright. We just want to keep each decade separate for now. These boxes are great to store memorabilia along with the photos, by the way—so just add as much as you want! If you need two boxes per year, that's okay, too.

It's okay, let it go.

As you're going through those photos, if they're blurry, or if they're 20 pictures of the same sunset, it's okay to throw them out (it's okay!!!). On a more serious note, a lot of my clients feel that they're throwing away not only a memory (even if it's hard to see—they still remember this moment in time) but the person in the photo is being discarded as well. I can't argue with this feeling, and I'm guilty of holding on to a picture of my sister and me where her eyes are open, and mine are closed. (My sister and I together in any photo is worth holding on to, even if I look like I'm half asleep or on drugs.) So, I get it. Just take those pictures and keep them in a holding area for archival material, or if it's digital, create a folder for these pictures that you aren't going to ever get rid of. It's all good. All I ask is that you don't mix the favorites in with the ones you'll probably never display for one reason or the other.

Once everything is in its box, pull the most recent box of printed photos out and begin there. Get those index cards again and write each year in that decade at the top (e.g., 1991, 1992, etc.). Take your best guess and place each group of pictures in the best year that matches what's happening. Use context clues like location, hairstyle, and clothing to help you. Do this for each box. Set up folders in your computer just like you did with the index cards, and remember to be consistent with your folder labels. Once you open those flash drives or look in your hard drive, you can start dragging those pictures into the right decade, then the right year. Now that you're all organized, decide if you want to scan your favorite pictures into a cloud-based backup system or if you want to just keep them where they are. You can share them a lot more easily if they're scanned and accessible to you quickly, but do what you're comfortable with. Either way, you're now ready to have fun with your memories!

Speaking of photos, I hope you're taking pictures of anything new you've bought, including art, jewelry, and electronics, so you can add them to your home inventory that you started in your 50s (nudge, nudge).

Attics Are Scary Places!

Indeed. Going into a place that you may or may not have been stuffing with Christmas trees, baby clothes (that baby is 34 now), and broken furniture you meant to fix someday can be frightening. Add dust, a critter or two that may have squeezed in there somehow (and has died), and a burned-out lightbulb, and you have a less-than-desirable place to spend a Saturday afternoon! If you live in a climate where the seasons actually change, you've probably avoided the extreme heat or cold, so if your timing is bad, and there's no time left (the house goes on the market in a week, for example), wear—or don't wear—layers and bring up some water (or hot cocoa). Before going "up there," make sure you have a plan.

- What will you do with what you don't want anymore?
- Will you have items to sell?
- Do you have a favorite charity, and should they come to you, or will you drop it off?
- Will you want to clean the space when you're done or leave that to a professional?

When you have those answers, and about four hours, grab a partner/helper, a flashlight, a few extra lightbulbs, your cell phone, and a tarp. The partner is for when you need to get things down to the floor below without going up and down the ladder each time. The flashlight is for you to find the socket to put the fresh lightbulb into, and the cell phone is for when you need to take pictures of the items up there to ask a family member (even if he or she is in the kitchen taking a break without you) if they want it or not. The tarp is for the floor below the ladder. If you have an extra tarp or blanket you were going to donate, you can use it in a nearby room for sorting. It's a good idea to move furniture around in that nearby room so you can bring a lot of stuff down—even if you don't get time to examine everything you bring down, at least you have it on a level of your home you don't mind going to.

Here's the other thing you should know: There. Will. Be. Dust. Use a mask! The beams are lower than they look—we use hardhats when we go up in the attic (you can get these at The Home Depot for very little money) and always check the floors for missing floorboards and, yes, holes. Holes are bad. If you see any signs of damage due to pests, have an exterminator do a site inspection before you go back up there.

When you're really ready to move and have chosen where you'll live, space planning is a critical step in the process. The numbers don't lie, and this is especially true with square footage. Often, when I'm getting ready to transition anyone into their new home, I do a floor plan with them to see what furniture and other decor will fit into their space. I keep in mind safety first and design second. If the square footage of a home (even their current home) won't allow two couches, we remove one couch and replace it with a smaller footprint like a recliner. Allowing space to move safely means less chance of a fall to occur and more room to use a walker or a cane. I measure existing furniture and use a magnet board to plot out each piece and where it will be located in the new place. You can also grab some painter's tape and "draw" out where the furniture will go on the floors of your new home if you have access to it. This has the most impact visually, and it works well to "see" where things will go.

When it comes to wall art, consider how much of your new home has available wall space. I've gotten to homes to unpack a new client's belongings, and they didn't realize there were more windows and doors in their new place than the old one. The art usually ends up getting sold or donated, depending on value and size, at that point. The hanging art you love (but no longer have room for) can be photographed or scanned and made into a photo album using web-based software. It can be enjoyed forever, even though it's no longer three-dimensional.

Cabinet space in your new digs is often underestimated as well, so measure the depth of each cabinet to make sure your plates, bowls, glasses, and mugs will all fit. Some cabinets are only 10" deep, while others have the standard depth of 12". Buying some Lazy Susans and Add-A-Shelf inserts for your kitchen cabinets will certainly maximize storage space!

How much space you need for clothing is challenging. Measure how much space your clothes are currently using in your closet; then see how much space is available on that rod in the new closet. Chances are it's about 50% less than what you're used to having. You can either reduce your clothing by half, OR create seasonal storage for your clothing, keeping just the current season and transitional wear in your new space, swapping out the items at the change of seasons. For storing wool items, we like using large lavender sachets.

CHRONOLOGICAL ORDER

L Having your home well organized and clutter free is the first step in making sure your HOME is a safe place for you to age in place. It's a good time to ask yourself if your aging in place plan is working. If you already downsized, are you able to get around and in and out of your home safely still? Here are other issues to take into consideration to create a safe home environment:

Top 10 Home Safety Checklist for Older Consumers (from the U.S. Consumer Product Safety Commission):

- Install smoke alarms and carbon monoxide detectors throughout your home.
- Have fuel-burning appliances, including furnaces and chimneys, inspected by a professional every year to make sure they're working properly and not leaking poisonous carbon monoxide.
- Have and prearrange an emergency escape plan with your family.
- Keep handy in the kitchen a fire extinguisher in case of fire.
- Install ground or fault interrupters, or fault GFCIs, in potentially damp locations such as the kitchen, bathroom, garage, and near utility tubs or sinks to avoid electrocution.
- Make sure there's good lighting inside and outside your home to help prevent falls.
- Make sure walking surfaces are flat, slip-sure resistant, and free from clutter and debris.
- Make sure matches and lighters are stored out of reach of your grandchildren. Keep all medications in child-resistant bottles.
- Keep all candles, ashtrays, hot smoking plates, and materials out of reach of children and grandchildren.
- Set your hot water heater to no more than 120° F to prevent burns.

Your Financial and Professional Goals

J We can't emphasize enough how important it is to review your will and insurance policies, reassign your Power of Attorney if necessary, and meet with your financial advisor(s) at the beginning of this decade.

I've changed my will **three times.** Life really does whiz by, and so do all the changes. About one month before your insurance policy renews, put it in your calendar to meet with your agent. No one ever really meets with them unless they need to buy a new policy. They go to networking meetings and make phone calls, but it will never replace how awesome it would be to meet with YOU and go over YOUR goals. You're not bothering them—you're making their DAY!

Regarding your financial advisors or broker, this is another helper you don't want to sit by the phone for. They typically only call you when they need you to sign an updated form or something bad is about to happen with one of your funds (maybe), and they'll need your verbal permission to move your money into another account. You'll need to be proactive here, checking in and scheduling your appointments, even if they're just phone calls. If you're not certain how to properly access your statements and information online, make sure you get help from your advisor to "get in and look." Really look, and really analyze. This is your money. They might be the expert here, but in the end, you're in charge.

In the jar or in the box? Ashes at sea or on a golf course? Do you want to be part of a tree's seeds? Okay, maybe these aren't choices you feel like making TODAY, but promise us you are making them soon. Since you don't usually get to choose how you're going to leave this world, you DO get to choose how you'll be, um...stored...after you die. I want my ashes scattered in Ireland, a trip I'll pay for, for my kids to take my ashy bits and put them into the Irish Sea. It's where my ancestors are probably from, but that's not the point. It's where I want my bits to go. I love the ocean, and I love Ireland. And I love my kids. I want them to get on a plane to Dublin, pop into a pub, order beer and a big bowl of (Irish) stew and talk about me. I'm sure they'll regale the locals about what an awesome adventurer I was, and of course, a stellar mother. Then they'll take me to the Irish Sea, do a shot of whiskey, and toss that stuff right in (upwind, of course. I hope they check conditions first.).

I don't mean to be morose or vulgar. It's just that it's going to happen. I know this. We all do, really, we just don't talk about it. Talk about it now, okay? If you can't talk about it, write about it.

When you pass away, there are going to be questions and uncertainty, let alone grief, from those who you loved you. They will need to understand your wishes, so it is truly helpful to answer these questions, at the minimum.

"My name is _____, and this is what I want done with my:

- **possessions:** _____
- **money:** _____
- **funeral:** _____
- **photos:** _____
- **digital rights:** _____

If you are looking for an incredibly easy tool to use, check out the "Peace of Mind Planner: Important Information about My Belongings, Business Affairs, and Wishes," by Peter Pauper Press Inc. It has easy-to-use forms for final thoughts and how you want your final affairs and possessions handled by those you will leave behind.

Your Relationships and Social Life

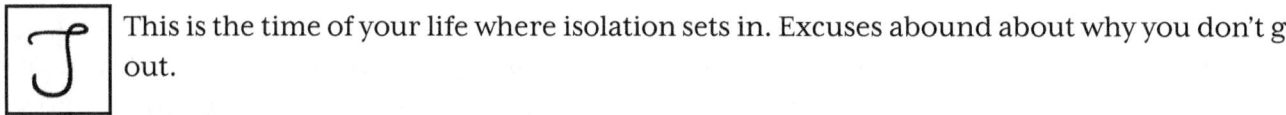 This is the time of your life where isolation sets in. Excuses abound about why you don't go out.

Being at home alone can be difficult. It's also a major contributor to depression and subsequently can cause health issues. When we start losing our mobility, it's easy to give up the good fight. We do this slowly at first, and then it seems to gain traction with almost any small reason that could contribute to how we're feeling. It's easy to lump these concerns into one large reason to either not go out and mingle with the world again, or to not have people over.

Grieving a spouse, parent, significant other, or good friend who's died is a normal reaction to stay home and take time to be alone with your feelings and regroup. And, it does seem that you're attending more funerals than weddings or otherwise happy occasions these days. This can grate on anyone's psyche. It's so important to balance these sad days with activities to look forward to, that are fun and light to fill hours with, and to do it in the company of those you care about. Depression is NOT a sign of normal aging, and you don't have to live with it untreated.

Yes, Jill, this is often the time that isolation and depression can become a struggle for many. Grief especially can be hard to deal with. If you've recently lost your spouse or life partner, you don't know how you're going to feel until it happens. However, there are some normal symptoms or stages of grief that may include:

- shock
- denial
- pain
- guilt
- anger
- depression
- acceptance and hope

It's important to know that everyone handles it their own way and in their own time. There's no right or wrong. It's been over two years since my husband passed away, and suddenly out of the blue, I'll just cry. On the anniversary of his death this past year, I was fine and actually happy knowing he was doing fine up in heaven. If, however, you haven't been able to lift your head from the couch or have been eating stale Cheetos out of the couch cushions, then it's time to get some help! Your spouse or loved one doesn't want you this way! To find grief support near you, visit www.griefshare.org.

The best way to honor someone's life is to LIVE!

One of the things that most helped me in my grief journey was having some defined tasks to do each day to keep me feeling productive. I actually found the process of planning a funeral as a way to get through the grief. It felt good to have tasks to do and to keep busy.

Chronological Order

There are a lot of details to be taken care of, but I had a checklist that helped keep me focused, and that gave me comfort and kept me out of overwhelm. I couldn't control my emotions, but I had some control over the tasks at hand.

When someone you love dies:

There are tasks that family members will need to take care of soon after the relative's death.

Immediately:

- Contact next of kin.
- Contact a funeral home.
- Arrange for a funeral or memorial service.
- Determine if the decedent made his or her wishes known regarding his or her funeral or memorial service, either in writing or verbally.
- Tell friends and family what the plans are. Ask them to help you contact people.
- Determine if all or part of the decedent's funeral costs have been prepaid.
- Submit an obituary to the decedent's local paper(s). You may want to include a charitable organization for donations if that's preferred over flowers.
- Make a list of everyone who sends donations, flowers, or cards so acknowledgments can be sent (FYI, there's no rule here. You don't have to send a thank you note; it's okay if you don't).
- If the decedent was a veteran, contact the Department of Veterans Affairs about benefits the estate may be eligible for (the funeral home should also help with this).

After the funeral:
There are several financial matters that need to be taken care of when a relative dies. However, you may not need to take these steps immediately. You and your family will need time to grieve.

- Get multiple copies of the death certificate (at least 5).
- Notify the decedent's attorney about the death.
- Find out if there's a will and who was appointed executor.
- If you're named executor in the will or by the court, contact witnesses to the will.

- Organize a meeting to review the will and handle the estate settlement.
- Gather documents: copies of the decedent's death certificate, birth certificate, financial statements, tax forms, list of debts, bills, life insurance, Social Security, and veteran ID cards.
- Notify the decedent's creditors. Close any credit card accounts.
- Close accounts or change payee on utilities and other monthly expenses.

Other steps you may need to take:

- Check into whether any homeowner's or auto insurance policies offer coverage during the probate process.
- Restructure any homeowner's, casualty, and life insurance policies, as necessary.
- Change the registration of investment securities by contacting the decedent's financial advisor or the brokerage firm, and make sure any orders are immediately suspended.
- Change the title on any property (including real estate and automobiles) owned by the decedent.
- Contact financial institutions to determine what information they need and how to change the registration on any accounts the decedent may have had.
- If you have any joint bank accounts with the decedent, have the latter's name removed.
- Review your own estate plan, including insurance policies, legal documents, investment plans, etc., and revise as necessary.
- File a federal estate tax return within nine months of the death if the estate's value exceeds the estate tax exemption for the year of death. It's essential to seek advice from an experienced estate planning professional. It may also be necessary for a final tax return to be filed on behalf of the decedent.
- Contact the employee benefits department of the decedent's employer to determine what death benefits may be payable and to whom. It may be necessary to provide several certified copies of the death certificate as well as other requested documentation.

Research benefits you may be entitled to.

Social Security benefits

If the decedent was receiving Social Security benefits, notify the Social Security Administration promptly. If you're the spouse of the decedent, you'll need to go to your local Social Security office in person. Bring the decedent's Social Security number, death certificate (a certified copy), and proof of relationship (such as a marriage license and the decedent's birth certificate). A spouse or any minor children who were living with the decedent at the time of death receive a one-time Social Security payment. A widow or widower can also receive monthly benefits generally beginning at age 60 or at any age if he or she is caring for an eligible minor (under age 16 or disabled). Unmarried minor children (under 18 or 19 if they're still attending high school) receive monthly Social Security benefits. If you're divorced from the decedent after a marriage of at least 10 years, you may be eligible for Social Security payments. Call the Social Security Administration at 1-800-772-1213 Monday through Friday from 7:00 A.M. to 7:00 P.M. Eastern Standard Time for more information on benefits for which you may be eligible.

Veterans' benefits

Call the Department of Veterans Affairs at 1-800-827-1000 to find the office nearest you or visit their website www.va.gov. You should gather the following documentation:

- The decedent's birth certificate
- Social Security number
- Death certificate
- Veterans Affairs records

Benefits going to a spouse and heirs may include pension payments and financial aid for education costs; it's well worth looking into.

My ex-husband and children's father, a career Army officer, died by suicide in 2008. He had been struggling with depression and financial despair for a long time. His sudden death was shocking and traumatic in its own right, but because I was no longer his wife, I had to work **hard** to have his family cooperate with the will. His brother was his executor and was in no hurry to put the will into probate. I had no idea what the kids, who were 13 and 15 at the time, would be receiving or what I was supposed to do for them. I did have recourse with the Social Security office, which was very efficient and responsive, and they helped me file for their death benefits right away.

His life insurance was paid out to each child through an annuity with the Defense and Finance Accounting Services (DFAS), and this particular arm of the government is challenging to deal with, especially if you have children who are in college and are still eligible for an annuity payment. There are documents that must be signed and authorized by their school's registrar's office at the conclusion of EVERY semester that proves full-time attendance of your child, and these forms must be filled out accurately and completely, or the benefit won't be given.

They're also not organized or easy to work with when they make the errors. In the years that each of my children graduated from college, DFAS claimed they paid an annuity amount that they actually never sent to my children via direct deposit. This matter was never resolved, and the kids had to pay more on their income taxes the year they each graduated college because, despite our multiple and frustrating efforts to provide the bank statements (showing no deposits) and correct documentation, they would not respond with a corrected income tax form (1099-R). My kids have given up getting this matter corrected, and I'm not permitted to handle it for them because they're the beneficiaries. We would call, be on hold for several hours, and as soon as we would connect and begin introducing ourselves, we would hear the dreaded "click," and that would be that! Every time they had to address

> it, it would just remind them of their grief and loss of their father. It takes a lot of energy to get what you need from this particular office, so make sure every "i" is dotted and every "t" is crossed on all forms and correspondence. If my kids decide to pursue a corrected tax form, and they expect DFAS to do this, they'll have to seek a case worker from their local congressional representative.

Insurance benefits
If you're the beneficiary under an insurance policy, contact the insurance company or agent to obtain the death claim forms you'll need to complete and submit. With the forms, you'll need to include a certified copy of the death certificate.

Retirement plan and pension benefits
If you're the beneficiary of any retirement or pension plan of the decedent, call the employee benefits department of the company that sponsors the plan and determine what your payment options are and what paperwork the plan requires you to submit.

Down the Road

Remember, there's no quick fix for the grief and stress experienced after the death of a loved one.

Take your time when making important decisions immediately after you have lost your loved one. You might make decisions that you may regret later. Rest often, eat right, and allow those around you to love on you a bit more!

About Your Parents

Some of you may still have living parents while still in your seventies. If managing their care has become truly difficult, it may be helpful to hire a geriatric care manager – to partner with you in a parent's care, and to advise regarding proper placement, and to champion for better treatment in a senior living setting or skilled care environment.

Advocacy is a beautiful thing. Do you remember the last time someone really fought for you?

My sister is four years older than me and is a good bit taller (like eight inches taller). Susan was never my best friend due to the age gap, and if I wanted to keep up with her, I had to learn a lot of things quickly, like developing unbreakable Monopoly strategies or how to do the Hustle on roller skates. My sister and I fought like dogs sometimes, like big brawling wrestling matches complete with pinching and hair-pulling. However, when someone ELSE threatened to put a hand on me, she was right there, just like a superhero. On one late spring afternoon in 1979, the perpetrator in question was a girl a year older and few heads taller than me, and she really liked to pick on me. I was short for my age (I still am), had red hair, glasses, played the violin, and was in the Girl Scouts.

If that wasn't enough, I was a bona-fide computer-programming, chess-playing, book-reading, skipped-a-full-grade-in-school nerd. When this angry young girl wasn't chanting, "Hey, Four-Eyes!" at me, she was making fun of my tiny school uniform, my shoes, my... everything. One day Stacey (not her real name, obviously I'm still afraid of her) loudly announced in the hallway at school that her sister could outrun my sister. My sister (who also had red hair) was a very fast runner, and was breaking records like crazy at her school on the track and cross-country teams. She was very popular at her school for this reason. NO ONE could outrun my sister. So, of course, I said that was impossible. I actually stood, hands on hips, and said that my sister was waaaay faster than her sister, and for some reason, it came to me to make a wager at the ripe old age of 10.

I told Stacey that if my sister beat her sister in a race, she would never get to bully me again. She triumphantly and boisterously agreed to the bet, and we set up the race for that Saturday. My sister agreed because not only was I in for a life sentence in verbal torture to the end of my days at Our Lady of Providence, but also her athletic ability was in question. The stakes were high.

That Saturday, in the lot of the Schnuck's grocery store parking lot, we gathered under the hot sun on the sidewalk near some metal grocery carts and the newspaper machines. It was like a scene from a Quentin Tarantino movie. My sister wore her "fastest shorts," and I had my Brownie camera with me to get it all on film. Stacey showed up on time, with her sister, I'm guessing, wearing her fastest shorts as well. I was going to tell my sister to wear her fastest shoes, but she was the athlete, not me. Some kid we didn't know very well held his hand up, and just like in the car racing scene from "Grease," or any movie, he dropped the little American flag (I think he stole it from his mother's front garden), and the girls took off. Watching that race was more agonizing than waiting to see if I passed my final exams at college, as it turns out. I think I was sweating more than my sister was. It was close at first, but then I saw Susan break out in a burst of pale, pumping arms and red shorts. My Razzles hadn't even turned into gum yet by the time my sister hit the finish line, where another kid was waiting with a flag declaring my sister the winner, and I cheered like I'd just found out I too was going to be tall someday. (I didn't. The pinnacle of my height reached a towering 5'0".) I was free. I was never going to be subjected to Stacey's insults or pushing in the cafeteria line, lunch money thefts, or sandwich-stealing antics again. And my sister went on to break more records at her high school than any other girl that year or many years after.

Now, THAT'S what advocacy feels like. My sister isn't a geriatric care manager, but you can feel like I did that hot Saturday in May. You can have someone fight for you and for your rights to receive co-ordinated and carefully provided medical and mental healthcare. A geriatric care manager not only makes sure you're safe but also protected.

What Is a Geriatric Care Manager?

A geriatric care manager can play a crucial role in assisting the caregiver of an older adult. They usually become involved when the amount of tasks related to caring for a loved one become overwhelming and complicated.

This certified case manager will meet with the client and family initially and throughout the continuum of services provided, developing and executing a plan of care that fosters open communication with all providers involved. Using the required level of advocacy, the geriatric care manager will ensure that the client's needs are fully met within the appropriate care environment, and will answer many questions that the client and family has.

Their services are usually not covered by insurance, so they are paid directly by their clients or family members out of pocket. This being said, most people that have hired a geriatric care manager, in our experience, have shared that it was worth every penny spent, as it relieved the stress associated with caring for their family member.

LIFE ESSENTIALS:

Things to have in place before you're 79:

- Updated Life Insurance
- Updated Wills
- Updated Living Will
- Updated Vital Records
- Updated Power of Attorney
- Updated Home Inventory
- Updated Health Benefits
- Updated Care and Living Plan (see Life Essentials Chapter)

YOUR EIGHTIES

Your Identity and Well-being

I would be foolish to presume I know what it's like to reach this stage of life, but I do know that if we rise each day and take a breath, we're living. You're here today, and you can make the most of it. Even if you've slowed down and need some support to get going for the day, you can still stay connected to your family and friends. Take the time to tell the people who matter most to you how much you love them, and spend as much time as you can sharing your wisdom and knowledge. If you're still blessed with good health, then be sure to continue doing all you love to do. Perhaps you always wanted to write a book—well, do it. Don't leave this earth with regret. You don't have to; it's never too late to accomplish a goal and see a dream fulfilled.

If you didn't take care of any of the items on any of the checklists in this book, put the book down, pick up the phone, call a family meeting, and get them done today. You no longer have unlimited time to do them. It's imperative you do them today! It's the greatest gift you can give to yourself and your family.

Take the time to share your story with your kids and grandkids. Write down the family tree, favorite recipes, and traditions that form the foundation of your family. These are priceless gifts to give to them.

Photographic Memories
Creating a family tree is relatively easy to do on paper, and can be fun to do with a software program like twile.com. I like to include the entire family, such as in-laws, stepfamily members, and anyone who you consider family. You can always do a pure genealogy-based family tree, with only biological lineage, on websites like Ancestry.com.

Before beginning, and if you are using the hard copy method, make sure you grab a very large piece of paper - like art paper - and a pencil. You may be doing some erasing! If you are using software, you may have to make a decision about the design of your tree. This can be fun, but also time consuming. You may want to map it all out on paper first, then digitize it later.

Where do you start a family tree? The best place to start is with YOU!

Write down the following information in a notebook or on a computer to get started:

- Your Full Name
- Your Children, including step-children and adopted children or children you consider your children by relationship
- Your Grandchildren, including step-grandchildren
- Your Great-Grandchildren, including step-great-grandchildren

That is the basic beginning. Then you can add:

- Your Parents' name (s) - this can be both biological parents and step parents if desired. This tree is about YOU and your family as you know it and understand it. Genealogy sites like Ancestry.com can help you create a more biological family tree if you would like.
- Siblings' name(s) - these can be biological, step and half siblings if you would like.
- Grandparents' name (s), including step grandparents too!

Finally, add on the extended family members:

- Aunts
- Uncles
- Cousins

> The tree is just the beginning! You can create a separate page or document in your computer for each person, and add more information like their geographic location (then and now) and interesting stories, making the tree fuller with each new mini-memoir.
>
> This is a different process than doing a DNA kit from Ancestry.com or 23andMe.com. DNA kits track your heritage based upon a small blood sample that you send in the mail. Ethnicity estimates and your ancestors' historical paths will be available for you to study. Many people have participated in these programs even further by electing to use their genetic data to find out how they can improve their health and determine the risks they may face for certain health conditions, based upon the findings.

 This might be the time where you decide to do the things you've always wanted to do "your whole life."

You might not be running a marathon, but you do need to move, so take a walk, ride a bike, or swim with some friends!

When we're honest about our limitations, we can bring in the support we need to remain safe and also prevent tragedies. As a family, sit down and take a frank assessment of your challenges and what you need to do about them. You can start here:

What can you still do?

Write it down here:

YOUR EIGHTIES

What are your physical challenges, and how are you handling them?

Challenge:

Strategy:

Challenge:

Strategy:

If you're still driving because you can, fantastic! If you're still driving because you can't or WILL not ask for help, then it's time to look to others and take them up on their offers. I LOVE being driven around! I drove for my job to sometimes four or five different locations a day, all over Philly when I was younger, and Pittsburgh later when I was in the second phase of my career. I was tired, frankly, of paying attention all the time and avoiding other drivers who actually chose NOT to pay attention at all. When Uber was invented, I was all for it. It made me feel rich! I remember asking my friends if they had only one choice of these luxury services, what would they choose: a cook, a driver, or a housekeeper/maid service every day. I was the only one in that large group who selected a driver. I don't see it as losing my freedom someday! I see it as a perk.

Chronological Order

As you continue to age, your memory may be showing signs of normal aging, or possibly dementia—even a little—might be creeping in. This is not the time to avoid it or make light of it. It's time to have honest conversations about what you're struggling with so your spouse or family can be aware and help you. Avoiding the signs will just cause more confusion and stress for everyone. As your memory continues to decline, it can be dangerous. Over the years in my business, I've had conversations with many family members who've reported to me stories like their homes being burned to the ground because Dad forgot to turn off the oven. Or they had car accidents, some that resulted in fatalities of others. And I've heard really awful stories about elder abuse because these issues were left untreated and the family was not only in denial, they were unaware of what dementia really was.

Remember, the top two reasons we end up in the ER are falls and mismanaged medications.

It's time to let go of your pride! Admitting to yourself and your children that you're having a hard time getting up and down the stairs or that it's too hard for you to reach the high cupboards in your kitchen doesn't take away your independence. In fact, what takes away your independence is AVOIDANCE! Denial is the fastest way for you to manifest what you fear the most. Avoiding getting some support with housekeeping or someone coming over to help you do the laundry, and falling down the stairs will be the fastest way you break a hip and end up out of your home and needing 24/7 care. Call your kids and ask them to help you figure out how you can now age in place safely. That's being proactive and reducing your risk of injury.

You may also have to accept that your home is no longer safe for you to age in. If you struggle to use the steps, then no home is worth staying in or worth the risk of injury. Pack up and move to a place without stairs that also has some services like housekeeping, transportation, and community activities with others. This is how we stay independent; we embrace the change and adjust along the way.

If you're still married and your spouse is sick, and you're trying to care for them, and you're in your 80s, you need to allow others to help you. Even if you're the pillar of health today, nothing will accelerate your own health decline faster than trying to be a caregiver at your age. YOU BETTER HAVE A FAMILY MEETING TODAY! GET ON THE PHONE AND CALL YOUR KIDS, and get the support you all need. Remember, you'll do no good to your spouse if you have a heart attack or fall from trying to help lift them.

Your Home and Your Space

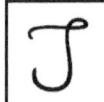 Still living in your home? Maybe you've already transitioned once, but now it's time once again to move, to take further steps toward a simpler life.

I'm hoping your health and mobility are allowing you to enjoy your home, wherever that is. This might be the time you have decided to move into a much smaller place than the last time you downsized. You may have moved into a two-bedroom apartment in an independent living community or a one-level apartment in your neighborhood. Now it may be time to move into a one-bedroom apartment nearby or even in the same community. This requires you to take a hard look at your existing space and see what you can part with as you once more shrink your living quarters to simplify your life. Hopefully, the first time you decluttered and downsized, you were able to evaluate your belongings for their meaning, purpose, and the value they brought you. Now that the new space will be smaller and more manageable, you need to plan well so moving day is a breeze and the disappointments are few, if any!

Being able to fully move throughout your home is key. If you're avoiding certain areas of your apartment or room, there are most likely good reasons why. If there are tripping hazards, or you're not able to access shelves, a fall could be in your future. And, once you fall, it's more difficult to heal at

CHRONOLOGICAL ORDER

this age. If you've fallen before, anxiety itself may keep you down, while you just move carefully from a bed to a chair to the bathroom. Please take the time to evaluate your surroundings for safe movement, and use the walker, the wheelchair, the stair lift, or whatever you're supposed to be using for safe, maximized movement in your home.

Your Financial and Professional Goals

Tips on Navigating the Healthcare System

Let's face it: By now, you may feel like the bulk of your calendar is filled with appointments and follow-up appointments to your healthcare providers. The annual checkups, blood pressure checks, blood draws, and physical therapy appointments are a lot to keep track of. Here are the best steps you can take to navigate your way through and receive the best care you deserve.

Step 1: Keeping a "Grab and Go" (Jill calls it this; she's brilliant!) file or binder is crucial at this point. Like the life binder we suggested earlier, this is the place where all your essential medical records, documents, and appointments are in one place. Believe it or not, keeping on top of this is just as important as taking your medications on time. It's a safeguard to your falling through the cracks of our fractured healthcare system. It empowers you to be the advocate for your best care.

I'll give you a few examples as to why:

You can't depend on the doctor to follow up with your specialists and make sure they send over the necessary lab results. You'll more than likely need to call the office and remind them to do so, or make sure it was done. They may say they're going to do it…and yes, sometimes they will, but oftentimes, it falls through the cracks!

Your primary care physician says he's going to fax over a referral for you to a cardiologist, and again it doesn't happen.

Having the "Grab and Go" will be the place you keep notes from those appointments and jot down what the doctor ordered, so you don't forget as well.

Here's what I put in my "Grab and Go." I take this with me each time I go to a doctor's appointment, hospital, or any other provider. Your adult children and Power of Attorney should know where you keep this in the event of an emergency.

My "Grab and Go":

- contact list of all doctors and pharmacists
- copy of medical insurance cards
- copy of medication list
- copy of living will
- copy of health history and immunizations
- copy of any test results
- appointment tracker/calendar
- notebook: I date a blank page for each appointment and jot down my questions and answers from doctors, as well as take notes of diagnoses or any conversations with the doctor.
- other: blood pressure log, diabetes log sheet, etc.

God forbid you suddenly find yourself in the ER; you and your family will be glad you have this. It will make everything go much smoother in an already stressful situation. Your family won't be scrambling to figure out what medications you take or what your blood sugar level was that morning.

Staying organized allows your family to be present and focused on being by your side, not rifling through your house looking for your Medicare Advantage card.

Step 2: Read that big book your insurance provider sent you! Do you know what your insurance does and doesn't cover? This is vital! Being blindsided by an unexpected medical expense or being billed for services that should've been covered under your insurance happens all the time. Don't expect the hospital or doctors to get it right. You need to know what's correct and check your statements. Know how many days your insurance will cover your stay in the hospital or rehab and what the copayments may be.

Today, many are being kept under observation in the hospital. If you're now in your 80s, it's pretty likely that if you're in the ER, you may be staying in the hospital a few days or then need to go off to rehab at a nursing home till you're able to return home. BEWARE: MAKE SURE YOU'RE ADMITTED, NOT KEPT UNDER OBSERVATION.
If you're left under an observation stay and not admitted into the hospital for three days, then your Medicare won't cover the cost of your rehabilitation in a nursing home. This has happened to many of my clients, and they were faced with $8,000 to $10,000 invoice for their stay in the rehab center.

Step 3: Know your options! Many hospitals now have what they call "preferred providers." These are service providers they chose to partner with to make things easier on them. They may have home healthcare agencies and hospice care providers they've partnered with. However, you have choices, and you can choose whatever provider you'd like as long as your insurance will cover it or you choose to pay privately. YOU HAVE CHOICES!!

Step 4: This is your life! You have the right to ask questions. The healthcare providers work for you. You can request a second opinion, and you have the right to refuse the course of treatment they suggest for you. Today many are finding alternatives to treatments. Do your research, or have a trusted family member help you before blindly doing "what the doctor has ordered." It may not be the best solution for you!

Your Relationships and Social Life

Believe it or not, one of the biggest tragedies I see during this season of life is a breakdown in families from the stress of never having the essential conversations and foresight to pre-plan for these last decades of our lives. If I could replay even one conversation I've had from an adult child calling me scared and sick to their stomach because her aging parents are living in a home that's unsafe and they're refusing to move or allow anyone to come in to help, you may wake up if you hear it. Sadly, the truth is it often takes several trips to the ER before any action is taken. And in our own stubbornness and unwillingness to be honest with ourselves, we then create chaos in our families. Stress, arguments, worry, strife.... Is this how you want to spend the last chapter of your life? I don't! I don't think anyone wants to create this, but we do by putting off what we should've done years ago. If you're reading this, you still have time to do something about it! PLEASE do!

Not all families are loving.

Sadly, here's another reality, and if this is you, then I would first like to say I'm sorry. No one should ever be treated this way! But the facts and reality are this: Elder abuse is real, and you may be alone, or the truth be told, your adult children don't care enough to help you. It's painful to come to this realization, but facing these facts enables you to prepare and protect yourself.

Trust me, there are even more ugly truths no one talks about, like the family who's more concerned about your wallet than your care who are fighting over their "inheritance money" while you're still alive lying in a hospital bed. I wish I could say this never happens. It breaks my heart that it does, and sadly it happens often.

This is why you need to make your wishes known and have a plan in place. Make sure you're protected while you still have a sound mind. Imagine if you start getting forgetful, how the people closest to you can take advantage of you. I can't tell you how many times I've heard conversations, or should I say horror stories, about the checks that were written to siblings or grandkids who are on drugs or the calls from some clients who told me how they were robbed by their own family and are now in legal battles. You must plan and protect yourselves.

CHRONOLOGICAL ORDER

Beware and know the signs of elder abuse.

The types of abuse and signs are as follows from the National Institute on Aging:

There are many types of abuse:

- Physical abuse happens when someone causes bodily harm by hitting, pushing, or slapping.
- Emotional abuse, sometimes called psychological abuse, can include a caregiver saying hurtful words, yelling, threatening, or repeatedly ignoring the older person. Keeping that person from seeing close friends and relatives is another form of emotional abuse.
- Neglect occurs when the caregiver doesn't respond to the older person's needs.
- Abandonment is leaving a senior alone without planning for his or her care.
- Sexual abuse involves a caregiver forcing an older adult to watch or be part of sexual acts.

What Are Signs of Abuse?

You may see signs of abuse or neglect when you visit an older person at home or in an eldercare facility. You may notice the person:

- has trouble sleeping
- seems depressed or confused
- loses weight for no reason
- displays signs of trauma, like rocking back and forth
- acts agitated or violent
- becomes withdrawn
- stops taking part in activities he or she enjoys

- has unexplained bruises, burns, or scars
- looks messy, with unwashed hair or dirty clothes
- develops bed sores or other preventable conditions

Perhaps you find it was you who was the abuser, or you look back and wish you'd treated someone you cared about better. Well, now is the time to reach out to them and tell them you're sorry. There's no time limit on an apology. Oftentimes people find that the person they offended in 1995 doesn't even remember the offense, and you've been carrying it inside all these years.

It's also important to acknowledge that the person may not be willing to accept your apology all these years later, and that's okay. Trust me, you'll have more peace about slaying your own giant and doing the right thing. Additionally, there may be people you're unable to reconcile with because they've already passed away or you've lost contact. I suggest you sit down and "write a letter and tell them what you would say if you could. This exercise is as powerful as telling them face to face.

Many studies show the effect that unforgiveness has on our bodies. A quick google search, and you'll find that 61% of cancer patients have forgiveness issues. That's an alarming number.
Other common aliments of unforgiveness are:

- Suppressed anger issues
- Low self-esteem
- Bitterness
- Anxiety and Depression
- Sleep deprivation
- Stress
- High blood pressure
- Heart disease

According to the Mayo Clinic, letting go of grudges and bitterness can make way for improved health and peace of mind. Forgiveness can lead to:

- Healthier relationships
- Improved mental health
- Less anxiety, stress, and hostility
- Lower blood pressure
- Fewer symptoms of depression
- A stronger immune system
- Improved heart health
- Improved self-esteem

If you haven't reconciled with someone you love, now's the time. When your memory fades or if you become ill, you may not be able to make amends or right a situation to invite the people back into your life who mean more to you than your pride. If someone has wronged you, take the time to forgive them, whether you do that with them or on your own. We're hoping you've done this before this decade in some fashion, but if you haven't, please take the time to do it now.

How do you share stories with grandchildren, friends, and family members? Invite them in, sit them down, and pull out your photos. Identify people in the photos, and supply as many dates and as much information as you can. This is your legacy, and it's important! When I organize my clients' photos, I'm always saddened to hear them say they don't know who the people are in the old photos, and since they don't know what to do, they either keep them in a box or envelope, or throw them away. One of my clients said recently, "Well, if I don't know who they are, and I'm the last one of my generation, then no one will know. This is terrible." And she tossed them into her trashcan. This broke my heart because those people in the photos will never have their stories told. No one will know who they were, who they loved, what they did, and where they came from.

It's our job to keep our stories going. Sometimes a curious family member might want to know more, but if no one ever approaches you, take the time and do it yourself. If you don't want to write, then record the story verbally. We have plenty of technology that allows this to happen easily, either with a digital recording on your phone, or using a tablet to take a video, or hiring a videographer to do a more professional job. No matter which way you do it, just please do it.

Companions
Whenever we begin transition services with a client, we ask about their natural support systems and if there's anyone they would like in the meeting with them, if their spouse or partner is no longer alive, or if they were always single, any friends? When we asked a recent client this question, her response was sobering and, quite frankly, not unlike ones we've heard before:

"No. No friends," she said. "All my friends have died. My sister is gone, my parents are gone, and even my younger cousins are starting to pass away."

It's completely understandable that if this is your situation, you're lonely and possibly a little blue. It's okay to feel sad. It's alright to feel lonely. What we don't want is for you to feel that you're all alone in the world. Maybe you don't have YOUR people anymore. But there are so many people who will care about you and want to spend time with you if you give them a chance.

One of the best ways to meet caring new faces is to care about people yourself. Volunteer all that knowledge and time you have to those who need you and what you have to offer. In his later years after his retirement, my dad volunteered at a hospital and read books to the blind and sick. He walked and cared for dogs at a local pet shelter and was on the Board of Directors for a community art center that he was passionate about in his town. He gave back so much of his time and enjoyed himself in the process. He also had a lot to tell me when I called because his day was packed with fun and interesting stuff.

My mom, a retired pilot, sold her profitable and successful aviation safety company about five years ago, and she actively mentors entrepreneurs in her small town. It not only gives her an opportunity to share her knowledge, but it helps someone who's struggling to learn how to run a company more successfully and grow the local economy.

CHRONOLOGICAL ORDER

If teaching and mentoring isn't your thing, try learning something new! There's still plenty of time to be the best version of yourself. If you didn't get a chance to write your life story or the Great American Novel, now's the time. With all the technology today, we can dictate right into the computer, and edit easily.

LIFE ESSENTIALS:
Things to have in place before you're 89:

- Updated Life Insurance
- Updated Wills
- Updated Living Will
- Updated Vital Records
- Updated Power of Attorney
- Updated Home Inventory
- Updated Health Benefits
- Updated Care and Living Plan

YOUR NINETIES

Your Identity and Well-being

If you've lived to reach your 90s, congratulations! You must be one special person who has a lifetime of knowledge to give back to the world. Perhaps you may be asking yourself, "Why the heck am I still here?" I truly believe it's because the world isn't finished with you yet, and there are gifts, talents, wisdom, and greatness the world still needs from you.

I'm always inspired when I have the privilege to sit down with some of my clients who are in their 90s. It seems to me they've mastered everything we've written about in this book. They've learned to adapt, grow, and thrive through each stage of life. They often have rich relationships and a great sense of humor. They're often givers and are always thinking about others around them. If they live in a supportive community, they're often the ones who are the most social and who seem to make everyone around them feel welcome. Remember, you're never too old to show kindness and compassion to others. Even if our bodies are breaking down, and we're one step closer to our last breath, we're still alive and have something to give. When we live our lives through this lens, we truly become ageless. It's my desire to live this way, to be ageless. I often joke that I'm reversing my age.... the numbers may be going up, but inside I'm feeling younger and younger.

You may have lost a little self-reliance by now. Nice people are potentially taking you to the doctor's, to go shopping, and to get groceries. You may have more things delivered than you used to, for the convenience and safety factor (not driving or walking too long of a distance on your own). Don't turn down an offer for a visit or an "outing"! Go OUT! Do STUFF! You're not alone. If you are still living in your own home, you could try to get involved in a senior community center. Senior centers are active, fun places! There are classes, indoor activities, nutritious food to eat, parties, and field trips (yes, just like you used to take in grade school, with a bus driver and everything!). Some even offer live streaming online classes if you cannot participate in person.

Nutrition is uber important right now, perhaps even more than ever. It's easy to keep eating sweets and processed foods because they are more convenient to buy and last longer due to preservatives. Eating healthy and whole foods, however, is still vital! Many nonagenarians might be saying, "I'm 95,

I get to eat whatever I want!" Ok. I can't argue with that point, but I will gently challenge that wisdom by encouraging healthy eating as often as possible. Including the following elements to your diet may get you past 100:

- Omega-3, which are found in fish like salmon, tuna and sardines
- Calcium, which is found in dairy products like cottage cheese and milk
- Fiber, which is found in nuts, wholegrain cereal, bread and pasta, brown rice, fruits and vegetables.
- Vitamins and mineral supplements like B12, C, D, and Magnesium are wonderful additions to your daily meals.

One thing you can do to ensure that you continue to thrive is to be sure you've checked off all the boxes of the checklists we've provided throughout this book. You're not going to live forever, and one day you'll no longer be on this earth. So again, I stress the importance of taking care of business so you can truly be present with your loved ones in your last days on earth. I also would strongly suggest that you have in place a designated healthcare advocate. This person can be your healthcare proxy who'll follow through with your care and any end-of-life wishes. You do get to decide how you want your last days to look like. You can plan a good death.

There's great importance in having a trusted advocate in your corner. Someone who will make sure that in the event of any health crisis, they know your wishes and will ensure that you're getting the care you need and your needs met as desire. One of the worst mistakes I've seen adult children make is to make decisions for their parents based on what they feel they would want without ever considering what their parents want. Your parents aren't babies. Stop treating them as such. Let them make their own decisions, even if you don't agree with them. Unless your aging loved one has a diagnosis of dementia or Alzheimer's, they can make clear and informed decisions about what they want and where they want to live. Don't feel you need to take over their lives just because they're now in their nineties.

If you don't have a trusted family member or friend to help you, then it's wise to consider hiring a professional healthcare advocate. They can come in with fresh eyes and see that you're getting the

CHRONOLOGICAL ORDER

proper care and follow-up you need. Most understand the complexities of the healthcare system and have the knowledge of how hospitals, rehabs, and nursing homes operate. They know what insurance does and doesn't cover and will make sure you're utilizing all the resources available to you.

I think it's safe to say that if you're in your 90s, you've spent some time thinking about your mortality. You've walked through a lot of experiences, and I would imagine you're wondering when your last day here will be. It's usually in this stage of our lives that we play the rewind button on the tape of our lives. Often, we seek to find the meaning of our lives. What was our purpose? Did we fulfill our purpose? This time of reflection can be a gift, and the end of your life experience should be shared as well. Open up about your thoughts, experiences, and wisdom. They're gifts your friends and family will cherish. If you can write them down or record yourself, that would be a priceless gift!

You may have feelings around your life experience that can take an emotional toll. Know that they're normal, and the people I've had the honor to see pass on to the next life have done so successfully and peacefully by facing these emotions as they did through each decade. They opened up and talked about them.

Fear of Dying

People are often afraid to die. Trying to figure out what about death you fear can help you face it and manage it. It will also help others be able to better support and care for you. For example, if you're afraid of dying alone, then letting your family know this and having a plan to have your loved ones with you in the end can be arranged. If you have no family, there are inpatient hospice centers where you can go and be surrounded by caregivers and invite your friends as well. If you're afraid it may hurt, then talking to your doctor and hospice provider about pain management, also known as "comfort measures," may also alleviate this fear.

Believe it or not, some people are at peace with dying. I'm not quite ready to think about it. But I do, often before I go to sleep. Sometimes I'm comforted by the type of day I've had, and I ask myself, *Was it good? What was good about it? Was I kind to those around me? Did I say what I wanted to say to others? If I had a goal, did I do my best to reach it?* Those elements of my day are important to me. I don't want to go to bed knowing I could've been a better person that day. I want to have that satisfaction in my soul that I did my best before I sleep. If I wake up the next day, I'm grateful for a re-boot, and I remember those questions.

Talking about your death with an end-of-life therapist or counselor can be helpful to not only confront your fears but to talk through some concerns you have about how to prepare for the end of your life. The feelings you have are real, and they can be tumultuous and frightening. Many people believe that seeing a therapist as they prepare for death is freeing, as it allows them to forgive others and themselves from the past.. Therapy also provides a healthy space to address some healing actions they can take during these last years.

Some of the emotions you may have, and some comforting coping strategies are listed below:

Regret and Guilt: We feel regret when we think we should have done something differently, or maybe there's something we wish we hadn't done at all. We then get stuck in guilt over these past regrets. There are things you might be able to do today to alleviate some of these feelings. Consider apologizing to someone for whatever you feel may have hurt them or your relationship. Maybe you can ask for forgiveness or forgive others. Most importantly, it's time to forgive *yourself*. You can't change circumstances that have happened, and some people may choose not to forgive you. Make your peace with that and let it go.

Anger: Few people actually feel ready to die, even in their nineties (remember, I said earlier, we never really see ourselves aging). It's perfectly normal to feel angry about your life ending. Unfortunately, anger often gets directed at those closest to us. Take a step back and realize that your being angry isn't going to change the facts, and do you really want to be grumpy and miserable in your last days toward those you love? Is that the last memory you want to leave with them?

Grief: Many physical and emotional losses come before the loss of life itself. This is its own form of grief over the life you can no longer live, as well as your family and friends, who are also grieving. They know they're about to *physically* lose you, and everyone is emotional. Talk to your loved ones about the grief and loss you're all feeling. The act of acknowledging the grief is often helpful. Staying connected spiritually as well helps many people of faith.

CHRONOLOGICAL ORDER

Feeling Lonely and Anxious: Even with many people around you, you may still feel lonely and anxious. Your care providers are there for you to be comforted, and the hospice team's goal is to help you be less stressed and at ease. Let the counselors help you feel more supported and cared for. They're there to support you—you're not alone in your journey.

Although there may be more physical and cognitive challenges, if you're in your nineties, you can still choose your activities, menu, dining and socializing companions. You can still decide where you want to live, even if you have limited cognitive or physical abilities.

[J] There are some great books on this topic that are comforting and informative. My personal favorites are: "Being Mortal", by Atul Gawande, "You Can't Afford the Luxury of a Negative Thought", by Peter McWilliams, and "The Conversation", by Angelo E. Volandes. Each book is different and offers valuable perspectives about the end of life.

Your Home and Your Space

[J] By now, I hope you're living in a simpler, easier place for you to manage safely. If you have downsized during your last move, you most likely have possessions that fit into your current space, which is hopefully on one level to avoid falling. If this is with family, great! If it isn't, that's okay, too. You can create a circle of care and friendship around you whenever you'd like, whenever you're ready, wherever you are. You could also possibly be living in a community with other people in your age group, who enjoy the activities and safe surroundings together with you.

I told my own stories about my possessions and their meaning in a photo album, sharing the meaning of the object in a tiny paragraph next to the photo of it. It doesn't matter how the story is told, as long as there's a record. I also encourage you to have a family meeting with the members who will be helping with your estate to communicate who should get what and why. The more we talk about our wishes before we...umm...go, the better off everyone is. There won't be laboring of decisions and guilt-ridden trips to the Goodwill if they know it's okay to donate the framed Casablanca movie poster (which you also happened to buy at Goodwill 30 years prior).

> When my 95-year-old grandmother and her husband needed to move into an assisted-living community from independent living, my aunts did a lot of research, using budget and location as a guide. They presented her with two options and took her to each one, letting her be in the environment, touring each community. They watched her reaction. Using her response and feedback, body language, and facial expressions, they were able to choose the right fit for her, and a few weeks later, after we downsized their possessions and packed up the boxes, they were settled into a one-bedroom apartment in a wonderful new residential community, loaded with activities and social opportunities that they both engaged in before they passed away.

If you're living with family, who are taking care of the household chores and enjoying time with you, ask someone to help you compile a list of your possessions and take photos of each item. In the list, describe the item, but tell its story, too. My mother keeps jewelry in the boxes they came in so she can write her story on the box of how she came to own it. For instance, "Pretty Pin from Jill: my 60th Birthday." The more information you can assign to an object, the easier it is for family members to know how important it is to you, and they can help you make decisions about who should receive it after we…umm…go. You can do this on the computer or in a notebook.

Space planning is still important so you can make sure all your possessions fit into your new, smaller space, **but safety is the major focus now**—making sure that if you're using a wheelchair or walker, it can rotate 360 degrees in any direction without hitting furniture or lamps or getting stuck somewhere. Removing those little rugs that are in hallways or in livingrooms means less risk of tripping and falling. Putting bars inside bathrooms - walls and tubs - are a way to create stabilization and balance while navigating tight spaces.

Having access to the items you need on a daily basis is crucial to managing your activities and interests in your home. For my clients who have trouble reaching higher than their shoulder level, I like to put lazy susans on countertops, in upper cabinets and inside refrigerators to allow my clients to have easy retrieval for medicine, snacks, glassware, mugs, and bowls - anything they might want to grab while holding onto a walker with their other hand, or sitting in a wheelchair.

Your Financial and Professional Goals

This is the time when we really do (usually) say goodbye to the people we love most in the world. Making sure our homes, our property, and our most treasured possessions get into the right hands is crucial now more than ever. Using an estate attorney to help you with the proper disposition of these items is advised, but there are many ways you can put together a thoughtful, legal division and assignment of property. It's time for you to make a final check of the will, insurance, and medical directives. Burial instructions and final arrangements must be made if they haven't been set up yet. Form a charitable trust if you have no survivors.

What's a charitable trust?

There are two types of charitable trusts. After you decide what assets you want to add to the trust, you have to pick one of the two types.

Charitable lead trust: After assets are added to this trust, a portion of its proceeds are immediately distributed to a charity(s) of your choice. You'll receive a charitable donation tax deduction, and the remainder of the principle will be distributed to your beneficiaries.

Charitable remainder trust: With this trust, you can choose to receive a consistent income that comes from all the assets you've added to the trust. You still receive a charitable donation tax deduction based on the initial assets added to the trust, but your chosen charity receives ALL remaining assets upon death.

Both types of trusts allow you to gain a charitable tax deduction which can greatly reduce estate taxes and eliminate the need for probate for your beneficiaries. Work with your financial advisor to decide on which type of charitable trust would work best for your situation.

Your Relationships and Social Life

My motto for anyone who's in this stage of their life is: "Let the sun shine in!" If there's a neighbor who frequently asks you if you need something or a nephew who's offered to run to the store for you—please let them help you. If you have someone at your church or synagogue who's suggested that they stop over or take you out to lunch sometime, take them up on their offer. Socialization is so important as we age. Isolation is proven to increase health risks, including mental health diagnoses such as depression. Being with people who care about us, and even with acquaintances who are in our card clubs and book discussion groups, will do wonders for keeping us in our homes longer.

Pride and stubbornness can be frustrating habits, especially at this age. Receiving help isn't revoking your right to privacy or independence. It's an art form that takes practice, and it's also an opportunity for those giving of their time to become better humans. Let other people spoil you during these years. Embrace the spirit of gratitude for your life and the people who care about you. If you don't have a large family, find a friend and make your own family. Create a network of caregivers and companions on your own—you're capable of doing this!

Finally, find an advocate for your well-being. Depending on your income, there are many levels of advocacy available. From geriatric care managers to administrative case managers in your community's social services office, someone can help you find the assistance you need. Many Department of Aging representatives from state and local government offices can direct you to the right resource for your circumstance.

If you're living in a senior community, use their technical tools to connect with your family and friends who aren't near your apartment or room. There are services that will come to you and help you use a tablet device or laptop to communicate via FaceTime, Facebook Video, Google Meet, or Zoom. There are also other devices specifically designed for easy video communication and a feeling of togetherness. If hearing is a challenge and prohibits you from making and receiving phone calls, you can receive a CapTel phone (usually for free) which displays all incoming words on a display window on the phone. There's a slight delay just like closed captioning, but it works, and it keeps phone calls as an option for socialization and support for older adults.

The best conversations we had as a family with my husband and children were within the last week of his life. I've heard from many of my clients that the week before their loved ones had passed, they seemed to have several days where they didn't seem sick and were mentally sharp. We experienced this as well. I like to think it's a gift from God. We were able to laugh a lot and talk about things we wished we would have more time to talk about or had talked about years ago! I was also able to forgive him and receive his forgiveness from me for the times where we weren't kind to each other. What I want to say here is this: EVERY MOMENT MATTERS. When we all near the end of our life, we'll wish we had a few more moments, even just one more! If you do what we've shared with you in this book…in those priceless moments of the time you have left on this earth together… YOU WILL BE FULLY PRESENT! To those of you who are in your twenties who stuck around and read this book… wow, good for you! May you make all the years count!

As I think ahead and I pray I make it through my 90s, I would like to leave this earth suit with a big smile on my face, knowing I lived my life well! I suspect if you picked up this book, you do too!

What will your gravestone say? I intend for mine to say,
"Laurean lived her life fully alive!"

Mine will say,
"I surfed until I died."

Things to have in place and completely updated before you're 99:

- Updated Life Insurance
- Updated Wills
- Updated Living Will
- Updated Vital Records
- Updated Power of Attorney
- Updated Home Inventory
- Updated Health Benefits
- Updated Care and Living Plan

THE LIFE ESSENTIALS

Life Insurance

Life insurance is a financial contract, usually between an insurance company and an individual. In exchange for premium payments, the company promises to pay life insurance proceeds (death benefit) at the insured's death to a designated beneficiary. Life insurance proceeds provide an income stream to survivors and help them maintain a certain standard of living. Proceeds can also be used for funeral expenses and college tuition.

There are two basic types of life insurance.

Term Life Insurance Policies
How it works:
Lasts until a certain age or for a certain time period (anywhere from one to 30 years).
When the term is up, you can renew your policy or let it end.
Benefits:

- Provides tax-free money to your loved ones when you die. They can use it to help cover your final expenses, pay off a mortgage, or as additional income.
- Tends to be less expensive than permanent insurance.
- May be able to be converted to a permanent policy.

Permanent Life Insurance Policies
How it works:

- You can't outlive the coverage as long as you pay your premiums.
- Offers different policies so you can customize your coverage to meet your needs. The four main types of policy options are:

Whole life: You pay a fixed premium (monthly or annual payment) and get a fixed death benefit. The policy also accumulates cash value, which you can use during your lifetime.

Universal life: Offers a flexible premium and death benefit. This means you can change the amount you pay if you need to. Most of these types of policies accumulate cash value.

Indexed universal life: Provides many of the same benefits as a universal life policy, with one key difference: the way interest is credited to the policy's cash value. Instead of being a fixed rate, the interest is based on stock market indexes.

Variable universal life: Combines the flexible premium and death benefit of universal life with investment accounts performance. Because these policies rely on investment performance, they may accumulate more or less cash value than standard whole life or universal life policies.

Benefits
Most policies build cash value. A portion of the premium pays for the cost of the coverage, and any remaining amount accumulates cash value. That money grows over time and can be accessed using withdrawals or policy loans or used to reduce future premium payments. Permanent policies offer tax advantages. In addition to providing tax-free money when you die, they also provide a way to grow your money faster in a tax-deferred account (the cash value). When done correctly, cash withdrawals from the policy generally aren't taxed, either. The cash value can be used in your lifetime. It can supplement your retirement savings or help pay for things like medical expenses or your kids' college education. There's no early withdrawal penalty, no required distributions, and payouts won't lower your Social Security benefits at retirement.

Why you need life insurance now:
There's no better time to purchase life insurance than when you're young and healthy when the premiums are most affordable. Your age and the state of your health (you're required to have a physical before receiving a policy) will determine your premium cost. The older you get, the higher the risk to insure you. It's that simple. You'll pay more. You may be young and single now, but that may change very quickly, and you might as well secure the best rate possible.

Many employers offer life insurance benefits as long as you remain an employee of the company. According to the US Bureau of Labor Statistics, the average worker will change jobs 12.3 times in a lifetime. You can't depend on that policy to protect you.

We strongly advise you to take the time now and meet with an insurance broker to learn more. At least attend an informational meeting to understand your options. Also, this is very important. If you do get insurance, be sure to ask your insurance agent about life insurance policies that have riders for long-term care. We'll speak more about this type of insurance later in the book.

Unexpected tragedies happen in life.

Some of you reading this book have most likely already experienced some type of traumatic event, directly or indirectly. For that, I'm sorry. By the time I was eight, I had lost my grandfather and 15-year-old uncle in a plane crash, and when I was 12, my mother was involved in a plane accident that resulted in several injuries and the death of her co-pilot and friend. When I was 15, my parents divorced, and my father moved away to another state. I left home when I was 17, just out of high school, and after only one semester of attending a college I had a scholarship to, I moved to Philadelphia to take care of an ailing grandmother. Life changes that accompany tragic events are challenging to navigate, and they happen to everybody, everywhere. At those times, I didn't notice that I was reacting to the events in various ways and that the losses were affecting and transforming me, not necessarily for the better.

I won't sit here and blithely say, "life happens!" Common phrases like that one may indeed be a quick and easy way to make sense of sudden changes and tragic losses, but they truly don't address the possible and somewhat painful damages done inside our heads.

Wills

If there's a WILL, there's definitely a way. You might be shaking your head a little here and saying that you're way too young to die, that you'll deal with this later. I had my first will written when I had my kids, so I was still in my 20s. I also got my first divorce in that decade, so I needed to update the will after the divorce was final so my children became my only heirs. (I love the way this sounds, by the way, like I'm royalty.) I was the primary caregiver and had physical custody of my children, but that didn't mean they would receive my estate or possessions or anything I wanted them to have. I had to spell that out in a legal will. This didn't take long, as I was young and had little to leave behind. But it was important to me to make sure I had plans in place for where my children would live after I died. Who would take care of them? Their father didn't want full custody in any circumstance, but not because he didn't love them. It had everything to do with his being terrified of raising kids on his own, and due to his high-demand, travel-focused military career, he couldn't truly devote the time they needed. So, I needed a backup plan. I had talks with my mother and my cousin. My mother would take them, and if she died or became incapacitated before they turned 18, my cousin (who is only three weeks younger than me) would take them and raise them. These were difficult decisions, but once they were made, I was much more at peace.

You may think at this point you don't have anything of great value that you need to even worry about having a will in place. But in the event that you're taken off of this earth at an early age, it's a comfort to your family to know what you wanted. Maybe you still have a collection of Marvel comics that you purchased every year at Comic-Con, and your little brother always admired them. Maybe you just hate funerals, and you wouldn't want to be stuck in a box with everyone looking over you and crying. You may wish to be cremated and stuffed in a firecracker and blasted off over the ocean while your friends and family have a party to celebrate your life (by the way, that's what I want to be done with my body).

Let's get real as to why. It's very likely that by your late 20s, you may now have children of your own. As Jill said, you need to have someone designated to care for them if they lose both parents in a tragedy. This happens, too. It's horrible, and it happens! If you don't designate who will raise your children, they could end up in foster care or under the care of a relative who you don't feel lives by some of your family values.

YOU NEED to sit down and write a will. Besides, we want you to start being comfortable embracing this truth: Dying is part of living. It's a big part of aging well to have a plan for the end of our lives on this earth.

By the way, you don't need to pay a lawyer to create a will. It's advisable if you have a lot of assets, properties, a business, etc., but even if you're still eating ramen noodles and sharing an apartment with three roommates, you can get it done for free! An excellent site for you to learn more and to create one is called FREE WILL.

Living Wills

A will (your last will and testament) is a legal document that explains exactly how you want your property and other assets to be handled after your death and includes family responsibilities, like naming legal guardians for your children. A living will tell your family what you want to happen while you're still alive and incapacitated to prevent those you care about from having to make hard life-or-death decisions for you.

Depending on what state you live in, a living will may also be called the following:

- Advance directives
- Advanced healthcare directive
- Directive to physicians
- Declaration regarding life-prolonging procedures

A living will is often just one document that spells out your wishes. An advance directive is usually made up of several documents such as:

- DNR (Do Not Resuscitate) order
- Organ and tissue donation
- Specific instructions about a diagnosed illness
- Medical Power of Attorney

No matter what your state calls it or how many forms are required, the point is the same: To let your healthcare provider and your family know exactly what you want to be done in the event you can no longer decide for yourself.

The following questions are answered in a living will. You may also address any other issue or medical treatment you do or don't wish to have in the document.

- What would you want to happen if you can no longer breathe on your own?
- If you can no longer feed yourself, how do you feel about feeding tubes?
- What types of pain-management drugs or procedures would you be comfortable with?
- Do you want a DNR (Do Not Resuscitate) or DNI (Do Not Intubate)?
- How do you feel about donating your body or organs after your death?

Most hospitals and physicians offer their patients a resource called "The Five Wishes." You can find a PDF version online that you can print off at home at www.fivewishes.org. The Five Wishes is an easy step-by-step process to create your own living will. It also includes a section to appoint a Healthcare Proxy. A Healthcare Proxy is the person you appoint to make health care decisions for you when you can't make them for yourself—sometimes referred to as a Medical Power of Attorney

Vital Records

What are vital records?

These documents are the most critical records that support your existence - they are your proof of life - not just for you but for those you care about. Vital records are documents that you will need to access in case of emergencies (both medical and financial), and may be required to apply for loans (such as mortgages).

Where should you keep your vital records?
I usually tell my clients to keep them "somewhere safe" since this is a place that only you can define.

Here are some good places:
- A combination safe in your home (the kind that's recessed in a wall or the kind that's too heavy for a bad guy or gal to haul out)
- A safety deposit box in a bank

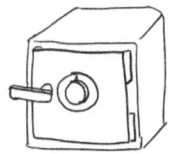

- A locked filing cabinet in a locked office of your home (information behind two locks is best)
- In a freezer bag in your freezer (this is a fireproof box of sorts)
- Scanned originals in an encrypted cloud account AND on an external hard drive stored in a locked vault or safe

Over 12 years ago, when I first started my career as a senior advisor, as I was learning how important it was to have your Life Essentials in order, I sent checklists to my parents and "trusting" that my parents were doing what I said. After my mother's health declined and my dad was diagnosed with lung cancer, I found out that the only thing they'd taken care of was having a will drawn up. They had appointed my sister executor of the will, but they didn't select a Durable Power of Attorney to address their medical and banking affairs. They also never filled out a living will. When I finally got my parents to sit down with all of us and get their affairs in order, my dad couldn't even find the will they'd made. After many months and several appointments with their lawyer and estate planner, we now have everything in order and created a binder to keep it all in place. My parents now have everything in one place in the binder, and my sister, who's now their Durable Power of Attorney, has access to everything she may need in the event of an emergency. Here's what we included in our binder. I encourage you to do the same for yourself as well as for your aging parents! We called it their Life Binder!

Copies of Vital Records:

- Birth certificates
- Marriage licenses
- Divorce decrees
- Death certificates
- Social Security cards
- Driver licenses
- Military records
- Will
- Living will (Five Wishes)
- Power of Attorney
- Healthcare proxy

Copies of Financial Records (location, contact information, account numbers, and passwords):

- Bank accounts (location, account numbers, and passwords)
- Copies of debit cards
- Credit cards (account numbers, passwords, and copies of cards)
- Investment accounts
- Contracts
- Debt settlement agreements (i.e. mortgage satisfaction letters)

Copies of Medical Records:

- Health insurance cards
- Medication lists
- Health history

Important Contact List (phone numbers, addresses, and email address):

- Next of kin
- Power of Attorney
- Primary care physician
- Healthcare specialists (all other doctors, dentists, optometrist, etc.)
- Attorney
- Financial planner
- Funeral director

Other:

- Title/deeds to property
- Life insurance policy
- Title/deeds to automobiles/equipment
- Loans or mortgages
- Safety deposit boxes
- Church documents: baptisms, etc.

Chronological Order

Power of Attorney

 By definition, a Power of Attorney (POA) is the authority to act for another person in specified or all legal or financial matters. There are four different types. Each one grants a POA a different level of control.

General Power of Attorney
A General Power of Attorney gives broad powers to a person or organization to act on your behalf. General Power of Attorney is an effective tool if you'll be out of the country and need someone to handle certain matters or when you're physically or mentally incapable of managing your affairs. A General Power of Attorney is often included in an estate plan to make sure someone can handle financial matters. Under a General Power of Attorney, your POA is able to:

- conduct financial and business transactions
- buy life insurance
- settle claims
- operate business interests
- make gifts
- employ professional help

Special Power of Attorney
Under a Special Power of Attorney, you can specify exactly what powers an agent may exercise. This is often used when one can't handle certain affairs due to other commitments or health reasons. Selling property, managing real estate, collecting debts, and conducting business transactions are some of the common matters specified in a special Power of Attorney document.

Medical/Healthcare Power of Attorney
A Healthcare Power of Attorney grants your assigned agent authority to make medical decisions for you if you're unconscious, mentally incompetent, or otherwise unable to make decisions on your own due to illness or hospitalization. While not the same as a living will, many states allow you to include your preference about being kept on life support. Some states will allow you to combine parts of the Healthcare POA and living will into an advanced healthcare directive.

Durable Power of Attorney

A Durable Power of Attorney allows your current POA to have Medical Power of Attorney when needed. Suppose you become mentally incompetent due to illness or accident while you have a POA in effect. To safeguard against any problems, you can sign a Durable Power of Attorney. You might also sign a Durable Power of Attorney to prepare for the possibility that you may become mentally incompetent due to illness or injury. You can also specify in the Durable Power of Attorney that it can't go into effect until a doctor certifies you as mentally incompetent or requires that two licensed physicians agree on your mental state if you so desire.

Make sure you have the utmost trust for whom you choose as your Power of Attorney

Trust is a crucial factor when choosing an agent for your Power of Attorney. You need someone who'll look out for your best interests, respect your wishes, and won't abuse the powers granted to him or her. Some families just revert to giving it to their oldest child or the oldest male child in the family out of tradition. However, it should be given to the person you feel in your gut will best represent your wishes, and that may not be a relative at all. You can choose a trusted friend, attorney, or other family members as your agent as well. The agent will be responsible for doing the following:

- keep accurate records of all transactions done on your behalf
- provide you with periodic updates to keep you informed or give an account to an assigned third party in the event you're mentally incompetent

You may also assign more than one person to be your Power of Attorney; for example, one can manage your financial or business affairs and one for any healthcare decisions to be made. However, you decide how these agents must act, either jointly or separately, in making decisions. Some find that multiple agents can ensure checks and balances against one another. However, this can also result in disagreements that can potentially delay important transactions or legal document signings.

Take all of this into consideration depending on your lifestyle and business affairs. If you do appoint only one, you'll, however, need a backup. Power of Attorneys can fall ill, be injured, or somehow be unable to serve when the time comes. A backup agent takes over only if needed.

You must be mentally competent when you sign and notarize the original Power of Attorney document. You'll need several certified copies to be presented to banks and other businesses to allow your POA to act on your behalf. Attorneys aren't necessary to execute a Power of Attorney. However, it may be wise to consult one for advice about the powers being granted, to provide counsel on what may be best for your circumstances. An attorney will make sure your document meets all the legal requirements for your state.

You can revoke or make changes to your Power of Attorney at any time. If changes are made, you'll need to notify in writing the current POA, financial institutions, and any applicable organizations that the POA has been revoked, changed, and a new one has been appointed.

Needing a Power of Attorney is as certain as death and taxes in everyone's life. Get it done!

I once got a phone call from a woman whose mother had just had a stroke. She was so overwhelmed and upset because up until this point, her 70-year-old mom was living in her own home, working a part-time job, driving, and was thriving socially on her own. In the blink of an eye, everything had changed. Her mother was now unable to walk, feed herself, or use the bathroom on her own. Her mental capacity was also compromised. She now needed care 24/7. The worst part of it was that because the family didn't have healthy conversations about aging, and her mother didn't have her affairs in order, they were now scrambling to get an attorney. Luckily, she was able to connect with me so I could help her. If this family had taken the time to do some research before this crisis and had gotten their affairs in order earlier, they all could have been present together with Mom at the hospital rather than sitting in a meeting with me. Seek expert advice early—you'll be glad you did!

Home Inventory

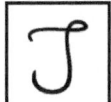 A home inventory is a detailed list of items you own. Period. Why do you need one? Lots of reasons:

- **Insurance:** If you have a claim due to fire, flood, or theft, you can easily pull this document and its accompanying photos up for your agent to use.
- **Organizing:** It stops you from buying more items and cluttering up your home because you KNOW what you HAVE.
- **Moving:** A home inventory will prove a useful tool when packing and heading to a new home. If you're not taking some of the furniture, art, and lighting with you, or are selling it, it's easy to adjust your list, removing and adding as you go.
- **Estate Planning:** Creating a complete list with financial values for your estate will go a long way when emotional bidding needs to occur when "the time comes."

Taking Stock

1. What do you own? FairSplit.com is a wonderful company that helps you take an inventory of what you own so if it needs to be divided as part of an estate, it's easy for family members to anonymously "vote" for their favorite items. In the meantime, your home inventory will serve to eliminate overbuying of stuff you already own, and in case of a disaster, it will help recover the replacement or fair market value of those items (depending on what's covered in your homeowner's insurance policy). If you have a Smartphone, tablet, or laptop, you're good to go with this online tool. It allows you to add items, their value, and a photo. It creates reports that you can send to your attorney, insurance agent, and/or family members who you trust. If you're not technically savvy, no worries!
2. Grab a binder, some plastic sleeves, some paper, and a camera.
3. Take pictures of your top 10 most valuable items, print the photos, and insert the receipts (if you have them) and the written description of the item, with as much information about it as you can. You can certainly take more than 10 pictures, but it's a way to get started.

4. When taking pictures, get up close and personal! Take pictures of any identifying information, like a serial number on electronics.
5. Take pictures of the item where it's normally displayed, in case you need to make an insurance claim—showing an item's context is often overlooked when photographing a valuable item.
6. When you decide the time is right to downsize and move, you'll have a great idea of what you have, which is half the battle of choosing what you'll bring to your new home.

Health Benefits

Understanding Medicare and Medicaid

What Is Medicare?
When you reach the age of 65, you're now eligible for Medicare. Medicare is medical, hospital, and prescription drug coverage. There's also what's known as a Medicare Advantage Plan. They're referred to in four parts. The information here can be confusing and it is wise to meet with a insurance broker who specializes in Medicare plans. You can reach out to your local Area Agency on Aging to find one. The following current information on Medicare is from the Medicare.gov website:

Part A (Hospital Insurance): Helps cover:

- inpatient care in hospitals
- skilled nursing facility care
- hospice care
- home healthcare

Part B (Medical Insurance): Helps cover:

- services from doctors and other healthcare providers
- outpatient care
- home healthcare

- durable medical equipment (like wheelchairs, walkers, hospital beds, and other equipment)
- many preventive services (like screenings, shots or vaccines, and yearly "wellness" visits)

Part C (Medicare Advantage)

- Medicare Advantage is an "all-in-one" alternative to Original Medicare. These "bundled" plans include Part A, Part B, and usually Part D.

Part D (Prescription Drug Coverage): Helps cover:

- cost of prescription drugs (including many recommended shots or vaccines). Part D plans are run by private insurance companies that follow the rules set by Medicare.

Your Medicare options include:

Original Medicare: includes Medicare Part A (Hospital Insurance) and Part B (Medical Insurance).

- If you want drug coverage, you can join a separate Part D plan.
- To help pay your out-of-pocket costs in Original Medicare (like your 20% coinsurance), you can also shop for and buy supplemental coverage.
- You can use any doctor or hospital that takes Medicare, anywhere in the U.S.

Medicare Advantage (also known as Part C):

- Medicare Advantage is an "all in one" alternative to Original Medicare. These "bundled" plans include Part A, Part B, and usually Part D.
- Plans may have lower out-of-pocket costs than Original Medicare.
- In most cases, you'll need to use doctors who are in the plan's network.
- Most plans offer extra benefits that Original Medicare doesn't cover like vision, hearing, dental, and more. Includes Part A and Part B. You can add Part D. You can also add Supplemental coverage. (Some examples include coverage from a Medicare Supplement Insurance (Medigap) policy or coverage from a former employer or union.) Part A and Part B; Most plans include Part D. Extra Benefits. Some plans also include Lower out-of-pocket costs See Section 3.

CHRONOLOGICAL ORDER

How do I sign up?

Some people get Part A and Part B automatically. If you're already getting benefits from Social Security or the Railroad Retirement Board (RRB), you'll automatically get Part A and Part B starting the first day of the month you turn 65.

Some people have to sign up for Part A and/or Part B. If you're close to 65 but not getting Social Security or Railroad Retirement Board (RRB) benefits, you'll need to sign up for Medicare. Contact Social Security three months before you turn 65. You can also apply for Part A and Part B at ssa.gov/benefits/medicare.

> Get help choosing the coverage option that's right for you. Get free, personalized counseling from your State Health Insurance Assistance Program (SHIP). Call 1-800-MEDICARE (1-800-633-4227). TTY users can call 1-877-486-2048. For general Medicare questions, visit Medicare.gov or call 1-800-MEDICARE.

You don't need to sign up for Medicare each year. However, you should review your Medicare health and prescription drug coverage and make changes if it no longer meets your needs or if you could lower your out-of-pocket expenses.

Mark your calendar with these important dates! This may be the only chance you have each year to make changes to your coverage.

January 1:
New coverage begins if you made a change.

January 1 to March 31:
If you're in a Medicare Advantage Plan, you can make a change to a different Medicare Advantage Plan or switch back to Original Medicare (and join a standalone Medicare Prescription Drug Plan) once during this time. Any changes you make will be effective the first of the month after the plan gets your request.

October 1:
Start comparing your current coverage with other options. You may be able to save money. Visit Medicare.gov/plan-compare.

October 15 to December 7:
Change your Medicare health or prescription drug coverage, if you decide to. This includes returning to Original Medicare or joining a Medicare Advantage Plan.

Please note: All information about Medicare was quoted and provided directly from the Medicare.gov website at the time of printing. Changes in legislation and enrollment dates can change from year to year. Please check with your local Social Security administration or visit Medicare.gov.

What Is Medicaid?
Medicaid provides health coverage to low-income adults, children, pregnant women, elderly adults, and people with disabilities. Medicaid is administered by states according to federal guidelines. According to Medicaid.gov, each state establishes and administers their own Medicaid program. They determine the type, amount, duration, and services within the federal guidelines.

The mandatory federal benefits are as follows:

- inpatient and outpatient hospital services
- physician services
- laboratory and x-ray services
- home health services

Chronological Order

Optional benefits are:

- prescription drugs
- case management
- physical therapy
- occupational therapy

Everyone needs to get educated on Medicaid eligibility in their state! There are things that your family can do earlier in life to preserve your family's assets. These financial decisions and asset protection must be done five years prior to applying for Medicaid Benefits. We're all living longer, and more and more people are outliving their resources. Each family is different and has its own financial picture to preserve. There's no one solution for everyone, but the likelihood of each of us needing care is certain. SEEK ADVICE NOW for yourself and your aging parents!!

Remember when you were thinking about how your Medicare or health insurance would cover the cost of long-term care, and I said NO, it does not? Well, you can see that Medicare is insurance for your medical expenses, NOT your living expenses. Assisted living and nursing homes are not HOSPITALS, so how do people afford to pay for living in an assisted-living community or nursing home? Well, here are some of the ways they come up with the money to afford their housing and care expenses.

Consider Selling or Renting Your Home
If nobody needs to remain in the home, this can be a valuable resource. Many times, Mom and Dad's house is a treasured place, and families aren't ready to take this huge step. If that's the case, consider renting the home, which will give the folks a monthly income that could cover the cost of assisted living.

Long-term Care Insurance: If you have a long-term care insurance policy, it should cover assisted living as well. If there's a policy designated for home care, it should be able to be used for assisted living, too. There are "facility-only" policies that cover care only in a licensed assisted-living facility or skilled nursing facility. Most insurance policies are difficult for the general public to understand, but knowing your benefits will be helpful in making sure you get what you paid for. It's common for insurance companies to decline payment on the first go 'round. Many times, you or an advocate at the assisted-living facility will need to contact the insurance companies and discuss these issues in order to get approval. To qualify, most companies will require that you'll need help in at least two areas of ADLs (Activities of Daily Living), such as bathing, eating, dressing, transferring from bed to chair, walking, and toileting. Long-term care insurance benefits vary widely depending on the policy. Benefits can range from $1,500 to more than $9,000 per month.

Life Insurance: When we think of life insurance benefits, we typically think that the funds aren't available until the person's death. But a life insurance policy can provide financial support now, if that's when the money would be most helpful. There are several different ways that policies can be used to pay for care while the person is still alive. Ask your life insurance agent about cashing out the policy, and about accelerated or living benefits. It can be called any of those terms. What usually happens is the company will buy the policy back for 50 to 75% of its value. The rules will be different depending on the company and type of policy. Some policies can only be cashed in if the policyholder is terminally ill; others are more flexible.

If the company doesn't cash it in, you can sell the policy to a third-party company in return for a "life settlement" or "senior settlement," which is usually 50 to 75% of the policy's face value. After buying the policy and giving you the percentage, the third-party company continues to pay the premiums until the policyholder dies, at which time the company receives the benefits. There are also options called "life assurance" benefits or a life insurance conversion program. This allows seniors to switch the benefit of a life insurance policy into long-term care payments. Life insurance conversion typically pays between 15 and 50% of the value of the policy. Although this is less than a life settlement, it's an option for lesser-value policies that might not qualify for a life settlement.

Reverse Mortgage
If you own your home and your spouse still needs a place to live, a reverse mortgage might be just the solution you're looking for. This allows you to borrow money on the equity you've built up in your home. When the last person is gone from the home, the money needs to be repaid, which usually means selling the home. This is probably not the best choice for a home that you want to keep in the family.

Bridge Loan

If you have trouble liquidating assets quickly, these short-term loans are an option and they're becoming more popular. They're usually available up to $50,000.00 and designed to fund the move to assisted living. They're usually used while waiting for the sale of property or to be approved for a pension.

Private Pay

Personal income or savings is the simplest route, but the cost of a month's rent can quickly use up your savings. You can also cash in personal investment portfolios, like 401(k) plans or IRAs. Often paying out of pocket is beyond what many can afford for very long. However, when all your resources have been exhausted, you can apply for Medicaid.

Veteran's Benefits

The VA (Veterans Administration) can be very generous when taking care of those who served. If you or your loved one is a veteran, you may be eligible for benefits that can be used to pay for residential care. If you have service-related injuries or disabilities, it will be easy.

But there's another set of benefits, known as "Non-Service Connected Improved Pension Benefit with Aid and Attendance" (Aid and Attendance for short), which pays toward the cost of assisted living. This is available to veterans or a surviving spouse who's disabled and whose income is below a certain limit. A veteran must have served at least 90 days on active duty and/or at least one day during wartime. The medical condition doesn't need to be service-related, but you must meet medical qualifications.

Aid and Attendance Pension for Veterans/Surviving Spouses

The maximum benefit amount for a veteran who doesn't have a spouse or dependent child is $22,938/year ($1,912/month). The maximum benefit amount for a married veteran is $27,194/year ($2,266/month). These amounts are current as of Oct 10, 2019.

People are often told that they have too many assets to qualify for the program. These folks aren't told that they could make some reallocation or adjustments to their assets without being penalized, and then they could qualify! Any time a person tries to "safeguard" their finances or assets, it can be quite tricky. You must make absolutely sure that doing this doesn't affect eligibility. It's also important to note that this benefit is a reimbursement for the out-of-pocket expense of care. You must be paying for care at home or moving into an assisted-living community in order to apply. You'll need to apply through the Veterans Administration. Along with your military discharge papers, you'll need a valid medical condition that makes you appropriate for assisted living with a letter stating such from your doctor. It may decrease time in the office if you also complete the formal application form "Veteran's Application for Compensation and/or Pension." (VA FORM 21-526, Parts A, B, C, and D.)

Annuity

If you have sizable savings but are worried about outliving your resources, you may consider an annuity. When you purchase an annuity, you pay a lump sum to the underwriters, and then you'll receive regular payments over a specified time period (usually the rest of your life). This is one way you can stretch out your money and make sure you'll always have some money coming in even if you live longer than you expected. It's wise to have an accountant or financial adviser help you set up an annuity.

Care and Living Plan

This is the plan that you put in place for where you or your aging loved one will live. It is important to think about the many options and figure out sooner than later which is the most appropriate and preferred way to spend the last few decades of your life.

The descriptions below are provided to help you better understand your housing options. The following will help you better understand the services each option provides and the average cost. **Please note:** Prices will vary from community to community and state to state.

INDEPENDENT LIVING

You or your parents may want to consider independent living if:

1. You see yourself needing minor assistance with activities of daily living.
2. You'd like a place that doesn't require a lot of maintenance and upkeep.
3. You're ready to downsize and want to live in a safe community with people your own age.

4. Independent living communities are a good fit for seniors who are looking to move to a safer environment but don't require help with their activities of daily living like housekeeping, meals, and personal care.

Options include:

1. Apartments
2. Senior high-rises
3. Condos
4. Patio homes and townhouses

In general, the housing is friendlier to older adults—it's more compact, easier to navigate, and includes help with outside maintenance. Sometimes recreational centers or clubhouses are also available on site. You must be 55 or older for most communities.

Pricing and Payment: Private and Public Pay(low income housing)

- $400.00 and up per month
- Private pay rates vary from one community to another based on the size of the apartment and what they have to offer. Some include utilities, some do not.
- There are senior apartments for those on a fixed income(public pay or low income housing). Seniors must be age 62 or disabled and meet the set income guidelines. The rent is then usually about 30% of the senior's income.

RETIREMENT COMMUNITIES

You or your parents may want to consider a retirement community if:

1. You see yourself needing minor assistance with activities of daily living, but home maintenance is becoming a challenge.
2. You'd like a place that doesn't require a lot of upkeep and is easy to get around.

3. You like the idea of socializing with peers and having activities offered to you.
4. You'd like meals and transportation services.

Retirement living communities are a good fit for seniors who are ready to simplify their lifestyle and may now feel that cooking and cleaning have become a challenge. This is an excellent option for someone who still wants their independence but likes the idea of having friends and activities available to them in a safe and secure environment.

Services Provided:

- Chef-prepared meals
- Weekly housekeeping and linen service
- Activity coordinators who plan numerous events for the community
- Local transportation
- Units that include kitchenettes or even full kitchens
- Live-in management and/or 24-hour security
- Chapel services
- Onsite barber shops and beauty salons
- Concierge service

Some offer personal care services through outside vendors at an additional cost to allow for aging in place.

Pricing and Payment: Private Pay

- $1,800-$4,500+ per month
- Utilities, meals, most activities, and the above services included in rates

PERSONAL CARE and ASSISTED LIVING

You or your parents may want to consider a personal care or assisted community if:

1. You're now needing help with one or more of your activities of daily living (the things we normally do): help with meals, housekeeping, laundry, bathing, dressing, and driving.
2. You have a decline in your mobility and are feeling unsteady on your feet. Stairs and getting in and out of the shower are now becoming a challenge.
3. You're feeling a little more forgetful and having a hard time remembering to take your medication and manage your finances.
4. You'd like the peace of mind knowing there's help 24 hours a day, 7 days a week. You won't be alone.
5. Your doctor, family, and friends are concerned about your being alone.

Personal care and assisted-living communities are great options for seniors who now need extra support on a regular basis. The goal of a personal care and assisted-living community is to offer the support you need as you age but to respect your independence and help keep you safe and thriving. Some communities can provide a higher level of care for their residents than others, so it's important to evaluate what your current and future needs may be before deciding. Most communities offer different-sized units with kitchenettes ranging in size from a studio to a two-bedroom. Many communities also offer shared room rates for those needing a more cost-effective option.

Services provided in most communities:

- Staff available 24/7 to meet scheduled and unscheduled needs
- Care overseen by an RN and certified caregivers to assist with all activities of daily living as needed
- 24/7 security and emergency response systems
- Chef-prepared meals and snacks in the community dining room
- Weekly housekeeping and linen services provided
- Laundry service provided

- Pharmacy, visiting physicians, podiatrist, physical therapy services, and exercise and wellness programs offered on site at most communities
- Local transportation
- Communities are well designed to meet your needs, and most have walk-in showers, handrails, elevators, and nonskid flooring to keep you safe
- Activity coordinators that plan daily programs and special events
- Chapel services
- Onsite barber shops, beauty salons, and other common areas like cafés, theaters, libraries, fitness centers, and community gardens
- Concierge service

Pricing and Payment: Private Pay

- $2,000-$6,000+ per month
- Currently, the average starting cost for a private room in a personal care and assisted living community is about $3,500 per month.
- Cost is determined by the following:
  - Size of the unit you choose
  - Amount of help you need
- At most communities, there are fees for the different levels of care. Be sure to ask about this. Room rates usually include all utilities, meals, snacks, housekeeping, and laundry services.

NURSING HOMES

You or your parents may want to consider a nursing home if:

1. You're now needing help with all your activities of daily living (the things we normally do): help with meals, housekeeping, laundry, bathing, dressing, driving; you have a medical need, and you need your care overseen by a doctor and nurses daily
2. You're in need of rehabilitation from surgery or illness
3. Your doctor has recommended this level of care

Nursing homes, also known as long-term skilled nursing homes, offer the highest level of care outside of a hospital. Many seniors will go to a nursing home for a short-term rehabilitation stay after surgery or illness. Nursing homes provide 24-hour nursing and medical care for those with chronic long-term illnesses. Regular medical supervision is necessary for the resident.

Services Provided:

- 24/7 'round-the-clock nursing staff
- A licensed physician who supervises each patient's care
- Room, board, meals, and activities on site
- Occupational therapists on site
- Physical therapists on site
- Speech therapy on site
- Other medically necessary care such as wound care, infection control, respiratory therapy, IV treatments, special diets, hospice care, and more at most homes

Pricing and Payment: Private Pay, Medicare, Medicaid, and Private Insurance*

- $8,000.00+ per month
- Medicare only covers limited stays in nursing homes. Skilled nursing or rehabilitation services are covered for a period of about 100 days after a hospitalization.
- If your income and assets are limited, you may qualify for medical assistance known as Medicaid.

CCRC-Continuum of Care Retirement Community
You or your parents may want to consider a CCRC if:

1. You're ready to downsize and want to live in a safe community with people your own age
2. You desire a community that offers a progression in care when needed so you can age in place
3. You're looking for a carefree lifestyle that doesn't require a lot of maintenance and offers a variety of services and amenities

CCRC communities are excellent options for those who are retired and are looking for a worry-free lifestyle as they age. CCRC communities offer all the senior housing options all on one campus. Most campus communities offer a large variety of housing options, from independent living apartments, patio homes, and townhouses, to assisted-living, memory care, and skilled nursing care.

Services Provided:
All the services of retirement communities, personal care, and assisted-living homes, and skilled nursing care on one campus

Pricing and Payment: Private and Public Pay*
CCRC communities offer a variety of options for payment. Most communities require a "buy-in fee" or "endowment" to enter the community. Some communities do offer month-to-month options. It's best to speak directly with the community you're interested in to learn more about the buy-in fees and/or entrance fees as well as monthly rates to reside in the community. These fees vary greatly from one community to another.

It's Time to Start Touring
The best advice is to locate and visit assisted-living communities before a crisis. Meeting the staff, residents, and often family members are some of the best ways to learn about the community. Every assisted-living community is unique, but there are common questions to ask yourself and the community before, during, and after a visit. The checklist that follows will help you ask these questions and make an assessment for yourself and/or a loved one. It's never too early to visit.

It's best to schedule an appointment to tour a community. When you set an appointment, you'll then meet with the appropriate person who will take the time to answer all your questions and give you their undivided attention. Plan on your visit to be about an hour long.

It's important to find an environment where you or your loved one will feel most comfortable. Some communities are very beautiful, and often you can be "blown away" by the decor and furnishings. But this will be your new home, and you may feel more comfortable in a place that's less fancy. It's important to look for a place where you know you or your loved one can feel the most like themselves. The most expensive communities don't always provide the best care and attention. Look beyond the decorations!

What to look for and what to ask when you visit:

Environment:

- As you arrive at the community, do you like its location and outward appearance?
- As you enter the lobby and tour the community, is the décor attractive and homelike?
- Do you receive a warm greeting from staff welcoming you to the community?
- Do residents socialize with each other and appear happy and comfortable?
- Does the executive director call residents by name and interact warmly with them as you tour the community?
- Are you able to talk with residents about how they like the community and staff?
- Do the staff members treat each other in a professional manner?
- Are the staff members whom you pass during your tour friendly to you?
- Are visits with the resident welcome at any time?

Physical Features:

- Is the community well designed for your needs?
- Are doorways, hallways, and rooms accommodating to wheelchairs and walkers?

- Is the community clean, free of odors, and appropriately heated/cooled?
- Does the community have sprinklers, smoke detectors, and clearly marked exits?
- Are elevators available for those unable to use stairways?
- Are cupboards and shelves easy to reach?
- Does the community have good natural and artificial lighting?

Service and Amenities:

- Can the community provide a list of care services and amenities available?
- Is there a nurse on staff?
- Is staff available to provide 24-hour assistance with activities of daily living?
- What are the training requirements for staff?
- Does the community provide housekeeping services in personal living spaces?
- Does the community provide scheduled transportation to doctors' offices, the hairdresser, shopping, and other activities desired by residents?
- Are barber/beautician services offered on site?

Residency, Cost, and Care:

- Is there a written plan of care for each resident? How frequently is it reviewed and updated?
- Is a residency agreement available for review before move-in?
- Is a consumer disclosure form available that discloses personal care and supportive services, all fees, as well as move-in and move-out provisions? What are the policies for refunds and transfers?
- Are there different costs for various levels or categories of personal care?
- Do billing, payment, and credit policies seem fair and reasonable?
- Is the resident's bill of rights posted?

Dining, Social, and Recreation:

- Do dining room menus vary from day to day and meal to meal?
- Are snacks available?
- Can the community accommodate special dietary needs?
- May meals be provided at a time a resident would like, or are there set times for meals?
- Is there evidence of organized activities, such as a posted daily schedule, events in progress, reading materials, visitors, etc.?
- Does the community create a sense of inclusion by encouraging residents to participate in activities?

Apartment Features:

- Are different sizes and types of apartments available?
- Are apartments for single and double occupancy available?
- Is a 24-hour emergency response system accessible from the apartment?
- Are residents able to bring their own furnishings for their apartment? What may they bring? What's provided?
- Do all apartments have a telephone, cable or satellite TV, and internet access? How is billing handled?
- May residents decorate their own apartments?

Other Questions to Ask:

- Does the community have a clearly stated procedure for responding to a resident's medical emergency?
- To what extent are ancillary services such as hospice or physical therapy available, and how are these services provided?
- Does the community have specific policies regarding the storage of medication, assistance with medications, training and supervision of staff, and record keeping?

- Does the community conduct criminal background checks on employees?
- Does the community train staff on elder abuse and neglect? Is there a policy for reporting suspected abuse?
- Does the community accept long-term care insurance?
- Is the state inspection report available for review?
- What are the most common reasons why a resident may be asked to move out of the community?
- Do volunteers, including family members, come into the community to help with or to conduct programs?
- Are residents' pets allowed in the community? Who's responsible for their care?
- Is there a complaints process for dissatisfied residents?

Resources

Aging
Expert Advice on Aging www.aginglifecare.org
National Institute on Aging www.nia.nih.gov/health/caregiving/long-term-care

Eldercare and Advocacy
Eldercare Locator www.eldercare.acl.gov/Public/Index.aspx
Health Care Advocate Locator advoconnection.com
National Center on Elder Abuse ncea.acl.gov

Finances and Legal
Free Will Creator www.freewill.com
Internal Revenue Service www.irs.gov
Personal Budgeting Application www.youneedabudget.com
Personal Finance Application www.wally.me
Personal Home Inventory Management www.fairsplit.com
The Five Wishes fivewishes.org
U.S. Department of Veterans Affairs www.va.gov

Grief
Grief Support www.griefshare.org

Medication Management
Automatic Pill Dispenser www.medacube.com
Medication Sorting and Delivery www.pillpack.com
Smart Pill Packaging www.qualife.co/cyco

Photo Organizing and Digitization
Digital Photo Plans www.nixplay.com
Forever www.forever.com
Online Photo Storage www.google.com/photos
Photo Prints and Photo Books www.mpix.com
Photo Preservation www.forever.com
Professional Photo Organizers www.thephotomanagers.com

Sources

Administration for Community Living. "Profile of Older Americans | ACL Administration for Community Living." Acl.Gov, Administration for Community Living, 2018, acl.gov/aging-and-disability-in-america/data-and-research/profile-older-americans. Accessed 1 Dec. 2020.

ADMINISTRATION ON AGING, and ADMINISTRATION FOR COMMUNITY LIVING. "FY 2016 Report to Congress: Older Americans Act." DEPARTMENT of HEALTH and HUMAN SERVICES, 2016.

Advo Connection Directory. "The AdvoConnection Directory of Private, Independent, Professional Patient Advocates." The AdvoConnection Directory of Private, Independent, Professional Patient Advocates, Advo Connection Directory, advoconnection.com. Accessed 1 Dec. 2020.

Aging Life Care Association. "Home || Aging Life Care Association." Aginglifecare.org, Aging Life Care Association, 2019, www.aginglifecare.org. Accessed 1 June 2020.

AgingInPlace. "Caregiver Burnout." AgingInPlace, 1 Nov. 2020, aginginplace.org/caregiver-burnout. Accessed 1 Dec. 2020. A blog article about caregiver burnout.

Buettner, Dan. The Blue Zones: Lessons for Living Longer from the People Who've Lived the Longest. Washington, D.C., National Geographic Society; Enfield, 2010.

Chronological Order

Centers for Medicare & Medicaid Services. "Medicare.Gov: The Official U.S. Government Site for Medicare | Medicare." Medicare.Gov, Centers for Medicare & Medicaid Services, 2000, www.medicare.gov. Accessed 1 Dec. 2020.

Eldercare Locator. "Eldercare Locator." Acl.Gov, Eldercare Locator, 2019, eldercare.acl.gov/Public/Index.aspx. Accessed 1 Dec. 2020.

Ferris Bueller's Day Off. Directed by John Hughes, Paramount Pictures, 11 June 1986.

FiveWishes. "For You and Your Loved Ones." Fivewishes.org, Five Wishes, 2010, fivewishes.org/five-wishes/individuals-families/individuals-and-families. The Five Wishes offers guidance through end-of-life decisions.

FreeWill. "Write Your Legal Will Online, Free & Simple." FreeWill, 1 Oct. 2019, www.freewill.com/learn/what-is-a-will.

Grief Share. "GriefShare - Grief Recovery Support Groups - GriefShare." www.Griefshare.org, Grief Share, www.griefshare.org. Accessed 1 Dec. 2020.

https://www.facebook.com/NIHAging. "Elder Abuse." National Institute on Aging, U.S. Department of Health and Human Services, 2016, www.nia.nih.gov/health/elder-abuse. Accessed 1 Dec. 2020.

"Memory, Forgetfulness, and Aging: What's Normal and What's Not?" National Institute on Aging, U.S. Department of Health and Human Services, 7 Oct. 2017, www.nia.nih.gov/health/memory-forgetfulness-and-aging-whats-normal-and-whats-not. Accessed 1 Dec. 2020.

Internal Revenue Service. "Internal Revenue Service | An Official Website of the United States Government." Irs.Gov, Internal Revenue Service, 2019, www.irs.gov. Accessed 1 June 2020.

Mayo Clinic Staff. "Forgiveness: Letting Go of Grudges and Bitterness." Mayo Clinic, 13 Nov. 2020, www.mayoclinic.org/healthy-lifestyle/adult-health/in-depth/forgiveness/art-20047692. Accessed 1 June 2020.

SOURCES

Medicare Rights Center. "Medicare Interactive." Medicare Interactive, Medicare Right Center, 2015, www.medicareinteractive.org. Accessed 1 June 2020.

National Center on Elder Abuse. "NCEA - Home." Ncea.Acl.Gov, U.S. Administration on Aging, 2019, ncea.acl.gov. Accessed 1 Dec. 2020.

Principal. "Life Insurance 101: A Step-by-Step Guide." Principal, Principal, www.principal.com/life-insurance-101-step-step-guide#step-1. Accessed 1 Dec. 2020.

Raitt, Bonnie Raitt. Nick of Time. Capitol, 19 May 1990.

Social Security Administration. "Social Security." The United States Social Security Administration, Https://www.ssa.gov. Social Security Administration, 15 Jan. 2020, www.ssa.gov/benefits/survivors. Accessed 1 Dec. 2020.

Social Security Administration. "Survivors Benefits | Social Security Administration." Https://www.Ssa.Gov/Benefits/Survivors, Social Security Administration, 15 Jan. 2020, www.ssa.gov/benefits/survivors/. Accessed 1 Dec. 2020.

The Photo Managers. "The Photo Managers - A Global Community of Photo Organizers and More!" The Photo Managers, thephotomanagers.com. Accessed 1 Dec. 2020.

U.S. Bureau of Labor Statistics. "NLSY97 Cumulative Number of Jobs Held from Age 18 through Age 32 in 1998-2017," U.S. Bureau of Labor Statistics, www.bls.gov/nls/images/nlsy97-cumulative.png. Accessed 1 Dec. 2020. This graph shows the average number of jobs held by an individual throughout their lifetime.

U.S. Census Bureau. "Census.Gov." Census.Gov, United States Census Bureau, 2010, www.census.gov. Accessed 1 Dec. 2020.

U.S. Consumer Product Safety Commission. Safety for Older Consumers - Home Safety Checklist. 1st ed., 4330 East West Highway Bethesda, MD 20814, Office of Information and Public Affairs, p. 16, www.cpsc.gov/s3fs-public/701.pdf. Accessed 1 June 2020. The Home Safety Checklist for Senior Living.

U.S. Department of Health and Human Services. "Long-Term Care." National Institute on Aging, U.S. Department of Health and Human Services, www.nia.nih.gov/health/caregiving/long-term-care. Accessed 1 Dec. 2020.

U.S. Department of Veteran Affairs. "U.S. Department of Veteran Affairs Home." VA.Gov, U.S. Department of Veteran Affairs, 2018, www.va.gov. Accessed 1 Dec. 2020.

Wonderlin, Rachael. "Alzheimer's Disease Is Always Dementia, but Dementia is Not Always Alzheimer's Disease." Dementia by Day, 7 Dec. 2018, rachaelwonderlin.com/2018/12/07/definitionsofdementia. Accessed 1 Dec. 2020.

Afterword

When Jill and I started on this journey together to collaborate and share our knowledge, we thought it would be a great little resource our clients could download off our websites. We had no idea of the POTENTIAL we had inside of us. What began as a small idea for an eBook evolved into a Life Manual. As we both took the time to intentionally plan, research, seek advice, and remain committed and accountable to each other, the more words seemed to fill the pages, and the more things we wished we had known earlier in life flowed out onto the pages. We experienced many things without having a clue as to what to do; we hope you won't have to be as unprepared for it as we were. The wisdom we've acquired from being trusted and allowed to be a part of so many families' lives through our work, we've imparted to you through each decade of this book.

I recently watched a YouTube video by Dr. Myles Monroe. The beginning of the video starts with this one question by Dr. Monroe asking, "Where is the wealthiest spot on the planet?" He then begins to tell you where it isn't. It isn't found in the oil fields or deep in the gold mines under the earth. Dr. Monroe says the wealthiest spot on the planet is found in the graveyards across the earth. Buried with many is their POTENTIAL! The ideas, inventions, books never written, songs never sung, records never broken, love never shared, are all covered and buried in the ground.

WOW! You're right, Dr. Monroe. Your video sums up my heart for each person who's reading this book. I want you to leave this earth with your grave empty! The grave robbers need not show up because you lived to your full potential; you left an imprint on the world. You released your brilliance that only you could share. You lived life, loved boldly, embraced change, shared your sound, and charted your course! There are no regrets, and the last breath you take will be with a smile on your face.

Chronological Order

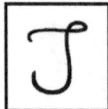 What is a well-lived life? Is it a life where we are good, useful or happy? What defines this for YOU?

Abraham Lincoln once said, "...and in the end it's not the years in your life that count; it's the life in your years." This former president had a tumultuous life, full of love, education, war, grief, leadership, political tumult, endless conflict and of course, history-making decisions. Oratorically, he is credited for encouraging reflection of ourselves, and for inviting us to explore the concept of being happy simply by making up our minds to do so. He also challenged us to explore empathy in our actions and open mindedness towards others. I would like to think that if he lived past his fifties, he would have shared so much more of his introspection on how to measure a successful and fulfilled life in the decades of one's sixties, seventies, and beyond.

I wish I could tell you that being engaged in life - being more involved with whatever it is you like to do - would help to reduce anxiety and create happiness for you. But sometimes making decisions to be happy and fulfilled has to be accompanied by a willing brain and a cooperative body. My most ardent wish for you, reader, is that this book has helped you to create your own happiness and meaning, in any decade of your life.

About the Authors: Jill B. Yesko

J Jill B. Yesko is a Certified Professional Organizer® and founder of Discover Organizing Inc., a firm based in Pittsburgh, Pennsylvania. She started her company in 2003 and has a team of professionals that help people to downsize and transition, organize their homes and photo collections, and specializes in working with those with chronic disorganization and who are living with hoarding disorder. Her first book, "I'm Right Here: 10 Ways to Get Help for Hoarding and Chronic Disorganization" was published in June of 2021, and is focused on shining the light on the several methods for accessing the right resources for these specific challenges.

Prior to running her business, Jill had a career in social work and human resources in a psychiatric hospital for children. She is a mother of two brilliant people: Nathan, her company CIO and Mary, a Geoscientist. She lives with the love of her life in Pittsburgh and is addicted to surfing, snowboarding and paddleboarding. She is a proud alumna of Villanova University and still dreams of going to law school or getting a PhD, in … something.

About the Authors: Laurean Kile

L Laurean is known as an expert Advisor to aging adults. She has helped countless families navigate the healthcare system, find suitable care and housing options. In the Fall of 2018 Laurean made a decision to sell her company, Patriarch Placement to pursue her passion of encouraging Faith Driven Entrepreneurs to release their full potential and steward their God given authority as Wealth Creators.

God has given Laurean the ability to help call out the seeds of greatness in others. Laurean hosts, The Launch Collective EXPO and Mastermind. She has a growing supportive online community, THE COLLECTIVE, where she leads monthly Lunch and Learns, book discussions and more.

Laurean currently resides outside of Pittsburgh, PA and when she is not co-creating with God, (while sipping a good cup of coffee with sugar free hazelnut creamer) on her back porch, you will find her engaged in conversations that include lots of laughter with her awesome friends (this may include wine, good food and a campfire). Laurean loves singing at the top of her lungs and dancing to worship songs. Laurean models intentional living and is savoring every priceless moment she gets with her adult children, grandchildren and family. She intends to travel the world and inspire as many people as she can along the way.

If you ask Laurean she will tell you she is a Professional Encourager and is blessed beyond to lead people into their destiny. You can listen in to her Podcast, "Release Your Sound with Laurean Kile" and connect with her anytime or request to have her speak at www.launchcollectiveexpo.com

Acknowledgements

Thank you to Laurean Kile, for being my patient partner as we volleyed ideas over the virtual net that 2020 gave us, solidified our thoughts, and created this book together. We truly wanted this book to be helpful to people as they went through the decades of their lives - mostly so they wouldn't struggle with the challenges that we had to overcome in our own years on this planet.

My parents were incredibly organized in their own ways, and helped me figure really hard stuff out when I needed them to, and even when I didn't want their help at all, they made me listen. Bill Banmiller, my late father, tried his best to help me with math, but our kitchen table tutoring sessions finally stuck when I started my own business. When the recession hit, both my parents (both divorced and remarried) kicked in some cash to help me along the way, and when the recession actually knocked me flat, each one had things to say, but none judged me for falling down. I found my way back, with some coaching by my mother, Anita Trotter-Cox. She is the consummate glass ceiling crushing business person we should aspire to become. She went from being a school teacher to a corporate pilot who pioneered in the flight safety arena, and retired well.

My kids, Nathan and Mary, both taught me to get my act together in more ways than one. From packing their diaper bags for their day care in record time while making sure I was actually not late for work, to ensuring that their high school yearbooks were ordered by the deadline to reduce social disgrace amongst their peers, I somehow pulled off parenting both of them. They made me a better person.

ACKNOWLEDGEMENTS

We are so grateful to our advance readers, those brave souls who had the guts to tell us what was missing from this book, what sucked about this book, and what was actually quite awesome about this book. They are: Paul Diana, Mary Yesko, Sharon Fanning, Linda Limberis, Joyce Phillips, and Susan Kemper. Laurean and I loved the critical input on the decades we haven't lived yet, and in Mary's case, that we had nearly forgotten about.

Nathan Yesko, my son and illustrator, created the cover for this book as well as the multiple illustrations that decorate the interior pages. He creates and designs all of our company websites and marketing materials without complaining, with dauntless patience, and always impresses me beyond measure.

Ethan Earlewine, our Content Writer (among many other roles he takes on) at Discover Organizing Inc., spent countless hours attempting to get an agent during a pandemic, then finally succumbed to the self-publishing process, learning how to use Adobe in ways his college English professors never even imagined. Ethan's kindness and support were invaluable to us. Also, we have no idea how to use InDesign, so he had no choice, really.

Sarah Quiqley gave this book its initial edit in 2019, and Andrea Susan Glass of WritersWay (www.WritersWay.com). gave it its last in 2021. We took the suggestions and made (most of) the corrections, and hopefully made them proud in the end.

And finally, a special thanks to Jan Blahut, the former Marketing Director at Discover Organizing Inc., who in 2018 told Laurean and I we needed to write this book when we thought a website "with helpful tips" was enough. We argued, she won, and here we are.

Chronological Order

L First, I must say, thank you Jesus. Thank you for this journey, for placing the desire to coauthor this book with Jill in my heart. Thank you for the creative ideas you sparked in us. The team of people you provided to support us and for the ability to see it to completion. Thank you for nudging my heart. This book is evidence that ALL things are possible with you.

I would like to acknowledge and thank the tens of thousands of aging adults and their families, other industry experts and healthcare workers who reached out to me for advice, support and collaboration over the years. Each one of you left me with a priceless gift. The insight and lessons I learned from each encounter with you has helped shape my ability to better love and serve others. The wisdom that I gained has been priceless and without each of you the pages of this book would not have been filled. Thank you for trusting me and sharing your lives with me. I am eternally grateful.

To my amazing children, Eyan, you have been on this journey with me. Thank you for staying out on the water with your mom. I know there were some scary storms and days when you wanted to get back in the boat, but you didn't and you also did not allow me to either. You never stop believing big with me! Thank you! Kailyn and Evign thanks for supporting me and encouraging me to keep on keeping on through so many changes. You do not know how much that means to me. I am proud to be your mother and You are all my favorite!

To my Launch Collective Tribe, may this book remind you that everything is born twice, first in the mind, So DREAM IT UP BIG and DO IT! I am eternally grateful for each of you who dares to believe with me. You all hold a special place in my heart. Together we are better and making an impact in the world. A most heartfelt thank you to my beautiful sister, Lynnann Voorhees, thank you for all you do for the Launch Collective, I honestly would not have gotten this book written without your continued help and love. Thank you for being all in with me!

To my besties and prayer warrior friends, thank you for always expecting me to be the best version of myself. For holding up my hands in prayer on days I could not. For speaking truth into my life and for always bringing joy into my days. I am blessed beyond with the best of the best friends!

A huge shout out to the entire team at Discover Organizing and special shout outs to Jan Blahut, Nathan Yesko and Ethan Earlewine. Thank you, Jan for scheduling writing sessions and holding Jill

ACKNOWLEDGEMENTS

and I accountable to a timeline. Your constructive insights and encouragement, I am so grateful for. Nate, your creativity brought the book to a whole new level. Every illustration made my heart leap with joy. Thank you for your ability to put pictures to our words and help with building a website. Ethan, thank you for jumping in and your willingness to tackle just about anything. Thank you for your love of the process. There was nothing you were not willing to do for us from research to final formatting. Thank you, Ethan. I am grateful to you all!

Finally, I am most grateful to Jill Yesko! There is no one else I could imagine would have been the most perfect person to write this book with. I have loved every moment of this journey with you, It was a pleasure evolving into an author with you, from dreaming up what the book would be about getting our ideas into an outline, writing sessions together at the library, zoom calls and especially that crazy day in a conference room writing for 9 hours straight because we were determined to make our self-imposed deadline(I could not see straight for days after, lol), it all has been a joy!

I want you to know Jill, you have forever inspired me to dream bigger. You are the real deal, witnessing how much you embrace every part of your life and journey as an entrepreneur. Jill, you are fearless and capable of anything you set your mind to. You serve and love above and beyond what is expected. You show up and set an example for others to shine too. I am blessed to witness your big heart and to call you, my friend. There is no doubt that your future will be filled with the most amazing experiences and that you will continue to create, inspire, give, serve, surf, write, and love deeply all the days of your life! I love you.

Index

A

ABOUT YOUR PARENTS 5, 36, 63, 106, 126, 161
ACTIVITIES 57, 145, 211
ADVOCATE 96, 225
AGE 2, 3, 4, 5, 8, 29, 30, 32, 36, 38, 41, 42, 43, 52, 55, 61, 64, 71, 72, 75, 78, 80, 82, 88, 90, 94, 96, 103, 114, 119, 124, 125, 134, 136, 143, 144, 147, 152, 158, 161, 162, 170, 171, 172, 182, 186, 189, 194, 195, 197, 206, 213, 214, 216, 218, 219
AGING IN PLACE 147
ATTIC 48, 49, 119, 120, 150

B

BASEMENT 15, 49, 73, 99, 101, 119, 121
BATHROOMS 147
BEDROOM 45, 71, 81, 88, 119, 137, 147, 171, 187, 216
BENEFITS 12, 63, 81, 127, 128, 131, 156, 157, 158, 159, 160, 195, 207, 208, 209, 210, 211, 212, 229
BUDGET 77, 78
BURNOUT 96, 97, 227
BUSINESS 9, 109, 154

C

CALENDAR 13, 19, 78, 129, 153, 172, 173, 208
CAREER 11, 12, 14, 35, 37, 40, 43, 54, 56, 69, 75, 101, 105, 129, 159, 169, 197, 200, 233
CAREER 9, 28
CAREGIVER 64, 80, 94, 95, 96, 97, 98, 136, 163, 171, 176, 197, 227
CHILDREN v, 14, 41, 42, 52, 55, 61, 63, 64, 65, 69, 70, 74, 84, 88, 90, 91, 94, 95, 99, 103, 107, 114, 115, 120, 123, 124, 125, 130, 131, 136, 152, 158, 159, 167, 170, 173, 175, 183, 190, 197, 198, 209, 233, 235, 238
CHRONIC DISORGANIZATION 50, 233
CLASSES 23, 104, 135, 182
CLEANING 24, 25, 26, 37, 56, 119, 123, 136, 215
CLOSET 14, 45, 46, 48, 71, 73, 75, 100, 151
CLUTTER 46, 48, 72
COUPLES 32, 68, 82, 83, 90, 128, 139
CREDIT CARDS 77, 79, 109

D

DEATH 72, 84, 90, 130, 141, 142, 155, 156, 157, 158, 159, 160, 183, 184, 185, 188, 194, 195, 196, 198, 199, 204, 211
DEBT 15, 22, 28, 29, 30, 52, 54, 55, 75, 77, 121, 127
DECLUTTERING 120
DEMENTIA 98, 107, 134, 145, 146, 170, 183
DIVORCE 11, 19, 68, 84, 90, 130, 196, 197
DOCUMENTS 19
DONATE 47, 100
DOWNSIZE 118, 119, 122, 206, 213, 218, 233

E

Education 9
elder abuse 170, 176, 223
emergency 29, 56, 136, 139, 152, 173, 200, 216, 222
Empty nesting 71

F

Falls 137
Family 9, 42, 146
family tree 166, 167
Finances 9, 225
financial advisor 55, 76, 152, 157, 189
Food 11, 109
friends 2, 14, 15, 32, 34, 35, 40, 42, 43, 44, 48, 51, 54, 56, 57, 58, 60, 62, 64, 68, 69, 70, 71, 73, 76, 79, 82, 88, 89, 91, 93, 97, 101, 103, 106, 109, 110, 111, 114, 119, 123, 129, 135, 141, 142, 146, 147, 148, 156, 166, 168, 169, 176, 178, 179, 184, 185, 190, 197, 215, 216, 234, 238
funeral 88, 154, 155, 156, 194
furniture 14, 15, 26, 31, 43, 44, 46, 74, 98, 99, 119, 137, 150, 151, 187, 205

G

Geriatric Care Manager 163, 164
goals 8, 10, 30, 32, 51, 54, 55, 56, 60, 71, 72, 73, 76, 101, 105, 106, 129, 134, 153
Grief 155, 185, 225, 228

H

habit 15, 16, 44
Health 4, 9, 38, 65, 85, 111, 131, 145, 164, 180, 191, 201, 206, 208, 225, 228, 230
healthcare 81, 108, 110, 115, 124, 127, 128, 143, 163, 172, 174, 183, 184, 198, 202, 203, 206, 234, 238
holidays 37, 44, 58, 78, 81, 88, 110, 111
home 11, 12, 14, 15, 17, 24, 25, 26, 32, 34, 35, 40, 42, 43, 44, 45, 47, 48, 49, 52, 55, 56, 61, 63, 64, 70, 74, 75, 76, 78, 79, 81, 84, 88, 91, 92, 93, 94, 95, 98, 99, 105, 106, 109, 110, 116, 117, 118, 119, 120, 121, 123, 124, 125, 126, 127, 128, 135, 136, 137, 138, 139, 142, 143, 146, 147, 149, 150, 151, 152, 154, 156, 164, 170, 171, 172, 174, 176, 182, 188, 196, 199, 200, 204, 205, 206, 209, 210, 211, 213, 214, 217, 218, 220
Home Inventory 4, 38, 65, 85, 111, 131, 164, 180, 191, 205, 225
hospice 141, 142, 143, 174, 184, 186, 206, 218, 222
hospitals 107, 174, 184, 199, 206

I

Insurance 4, 38, 65, 85, 111, 131, 160, 164, 180, 191, 194, 205, 206, 207, 208, 210, 211, 218, 229

K

kitchen 10, 24, 47, 70, 98, 123, 125, 147, 150, 151, 152, 170, 236

L

Laundry 11, 216
Living Will 4, 38, 65, 85, 111, 131, 164, 180, 191
loans 26, 40, 130, 195, 199, 212
love 8, 13, 14, 19, 26, 31, 32, 33, 34, 37, 40, 42, 46, 53, 54, 61, 63, 64, 70, 72, 73, 74, 76, 78, 79, 88, 90, 91, 93, 94, 95, 101, 103, 104, 116, 117, 124, 126, 134, 151, 153, 160, 166, 178, 185, 188, 197, 231, 232, 233, 238, 239

M

Medicaid 127, 128, 206, 209, 210, 212, 218, 228
Medicare 82, 134, 142, 164, 173, 174, 206, 207, 208, 209, 210, 218, 228, 229
Medications 138
Memories 5, 23, 51, 117, 148, 166
memory v, 20, 95, 109, 118, 139, 143, 144, 146, 149, 170, 178, 185, 219, 228
memory loss 143

CHRONOLOGICAL ORDER

MENTAL HEALTH 71
MONEY 2, 9, 11, 12, 19, 22, 23, 29, 30, 33, 43, 48, 55, 56, 60, 64, 76, 78, 79, 80, 94, 97, 114, 115, 116, 121, 122, 127, 128, 150, 153, 154, 162, 175, 194, 195, 209, 210, 211, 213

N

NUTRITION 182

O

ORGANIZATION 4, 16
ORGANIZING III, IV, 26, 45, 75, 117, 205, 226, 233, 237, 238

P

PAPER 11, 16, 17
PARENTS 5, 36, 63, 106, 110, 126, 161, 167
PHOTOGRAPHIC MEMORIES 5, 23, 51, 117, 148, 166
PHOTOS 5, 23, 24, 51, 88, 115, 117, 118, 148, 149, 154, 178, 187, 205, 226
POWER OF ATTORNEY 4, 19, 38, 65, 85, 111, 115, 131, 139, 152, 164, 173, 180, 191, 198, 199, 200, 201, 202, 203, 204
PRESCRIPTIONS 109, 138, 139, 140
PROPERTY IV, 22, 65, 131, 157, 188, 198, 201, 202, 212

R

RELATIONSHIPS 31, 32, 35, 60, 69, 72, 84, 90, 96, 105, 178, 182
RELATIONSHIPS 4, 9, 32, 36, 60, 68, 82, 103, 129, 154, 174, 189
RETIRE 76, 77, 114, 115, 129
ROUTINE 12, 13, 24, 33, 44, 70, 89

S

SAFETY 146, 152, 201, 229
SCHEDULE 11, 12, 19, 24, 33, 64, 70, 89, 99, 111, 219, 222
SELF-CARE 13, 33

SENIORS 107, 211, 214, 215, 216, 218
SLEEP 13, 26, 177
SOCIAL LIFE 4, 9, 32, 60, 82, 103, 129, 154, 174, 189
SOCIAL SECURITY 18, 20, 81, 157, 158, 159, 195, 200, 208, 209, 229
SPIRITUAL 9
STRESS 31, 36, 41, 143, 175, 177

T

TIME 2, 3, 8, 10, 12, 13, 15, 16, 19, 21, 23, 24, 26, 27, 28, 29, 30, 31, 32, 33, 34, 35, 36, 37, 40, 41, 42, 44, 46, 47, 49, 50, 51, 52, 53, 54, 55, 57, 58, 59, 60, 61, 62, 63, 64, 68, 69, 70, 71, 72, 73, 74, 75, 76, 77, 78, 79, 80, 81, 83, 84, 88, 89, 92, 94, 95, 96, 97, 98, 99, 100, 101, 103, 104, 105, 106, 107, 108, 109, 110, 114, 115, 116, 117, 118, 119, 120, 121, 122, 123, 124, 126, 127, 129, 130, 134, 135, 136, 137, 138, 140, 141, 143, 144, 146, 147, 148, 149, 150, 152, 154, 155, 156, 158, 159, 160, 161, 162, 166, 167, 168, 169, 170, 171, 172, 173, 175, 177, 178, 179, 180, 184, 185, 187, 188, 189, 190, 194, 195, 196, 197, 204, 205, 206, 209, 211, 212, 213, 216, 219, 220, 222, 231, 236
TRAVELING 76, 80, 116, 119, 124, 131, 148
TRUSTS 128

V

VETERAN 212, 213, 230

W

WELLNESS 9
WORK 3, 9, 11, 12, 13, 15, 24, 26, 29, 30, 31, 35, 40, 48, 50, 51, 53, 54, 55, 56, 58, 59, 60, 61, 63, 64, 68, 70, 73, 76, 88, 96, 104, 110, 114, 117, 118, 121, 122, 128, 129, 134, 136, 147, 159, 174, 189, 231, 233, 236

www.ingramcontent.com/pod-product-compliance
Lightning Source LLC
Chambersburg PA
CBHW082335300426
44109CB00046B/2487